For My Special Friends.
Bev & Buzz

Hope you enjoy this +
remember our special
friendship, which means
so much to me.

Ola Mae (Glascock)
Taggart

THE FAMILY:

100 Years in the Family of

James Edmund and Margaret Ellen

Glascock

By Noel E. Blythe

TABLE OF CONTENTS

James Edmund Glascock and Margaret Ellen Glascock, along with their children, Fred, John, Ross, Clarice, and Chloe

CHAPTER ONE

Life One Hundred Years Ago

On a cool day in the early fall back in 1912, a family gathered in a small rural town in the middle of Missouri. They were there with a purpose—they were there to celebrate the birthdays of two of the brothers. They must have enjoyed themselves because they decided that day to make it an annual event—a reunion of the family every year. Now 100 years into the future those of us who are their descendants know the impact that those people and this event would have on our lives.

The world we live in today is vastly different from the world that they knew in 1912— much more different than their world was from 100 years before them. Gone, probably never to return, are the quiet, peaceful lives on the farm that they led. It is quite improbable that they could have conceived on that day the tremendous changes that they would see to our world. In their futures they would see, as we have seen, incredible and rapid changes to the world. But would they—could they--have guessed any of it on that beautiful September day?

What was their world like?

As the calendar turned to the New Year in January of 1912, most of America found itself in the midst of a deep freeze. The winter of 1911-12 would be one of the coldest of the twentieth century. The bitter cold began around Christmas and continued through January and February without letup. The all-time record low temperature for St. Louis still stands from that winter—a miserable 28 degrees below zero. Even the summer would be much cooler and wetter than normal.

Winter's grip was broken by the spring in 1912 (as it is every year), and with it came the boys of summer playing—what else?—baseball. Three new ballparks opened that spring. Crosley Field in Cincinnati was the new home to the Reds. It would last through the 1960's before being replaced. Tiger Stadium became the home of the Detroit Tigers for the next nearly ninety years. And in Boston one of the temples to our national pastime debuted with its strange left field wall—Fenway Park.

The new stadium bode well for the Sox. They opened the season with a win against the Highlanders in New York where their rivals sported a new look—pinstripes. That iconic look still lives today with the Highlander's successors—the Yankees. But this was the year for the Sox, as they won 105 games and easily took the American League Pennant. Over in the National League the New York Giants won 103 and outdistanced all their rivals. They meet in the World Series, with the Sox finally beating the Giants in eight games. Game two it seems, was a tie.

1912 also featured another of our peculiar American institutions—a presidential election. And this one was unlike anything those of us alive today have ever experienced!

Incumbent Republican president William Howard Taft was nominated by the GOP to carry their banner again. This infuriated former president Teddy Roosevelt who was gravely disappointed in his protégé and ran against him for the nomination. Roosevelt, the progressive, broke with the conservative Republicans of Taft and formed the Bull Moose Party. Roosevelt accepted their nomination. To make matters worse for President Taft, Vice-President James Sherman died while campaigning in his native New York. The split and dissension among the Republicans opened the way for the Democrats.

Missouri's own Champ Clark, the Speaker of the House, was the odds on favorite to be nominated by the Democrats, and he held a majority of votes in the early balloting. But the Democratic convention rules insisted upon a 2/3 majority—which Clark didn't have. Then the Tamney Hall political machine from New York threw their support to Clark.

This caused many of the progressives in the party to immediately reject Clark and move toward New Jersey governor Woodrow Wilson. The tide had turned and Wilson eventually received the nomination. The fall campaign would be bitter. But the divided Republicans made it easy for Wilson to win in a landslide. The newly elected president became only one of two Democratic presidents from 1860 until 1932.

1912 brought several unusual occurrences. In June, Mount Novarupta in Alaska erupted and nearly buried Kodiak, Alaska in ash. A meteorite stuck near Holbrook, Arizona in July. And one of the biggest hoaxes in the history of science was perpetrated when Charles Dawson announced he had discovered "Piltdown Man" in a gravel pit. It would take forty years, but later investigation would find that the "discovery" was simply a clever fraud.

The United States grew by two states in 1912. New Mexico was admitted as the 47th state in January, while neighboring Arizona followed as the 48th state in February. The entire budget for the federal government totaled just $690 million dollars for the year. Unemployment stood at 4.6% while the cost of a first class stamp was just two cents. Congress would extend the 8-hour workday to all federal employees in 1912. Most workers in private industry remained on 10- and 12-hour workdays. And the cherry trees were replanted in Washington, D.C. by first lady Helen Taft to replace those killed from an infestation of insects and disease.

Up in Maine, a new store was opened by owner L. L. Bean featuring hunting and outdoor clothing. His creation, the Maine Hunting Boot, was his headline product. The Nabisco Company would introduce the "Oreo Biscuit" that year, while "Ocean Spray Cranberry Sauce" was the newest product from the Cape Cod Cannery Company. Morton's Table Salt was repackaged in a blue & white paper canister with an aluminum pour spout. And in California two new self-service grocery stores opened—the first of their kind in the world.

An organization which will become known as the Girl Scouts began in Savannah, Georgia, when a troop of 18 girls was formed. Author Zane Gray published perhaps his best known novel, "Riders of the Purple Sage," while *All-Story* magazine would publish a new story by unknown author Edgar Rice Burroughs called, "Tarzan, Lord of the Apes." W. C. Handy published the song "The Memphis Blues," the first blues song. And Methodist songwriter C. Austin Miles published his classic hymn, "In the Garden."

The America of 1912, particularly in places like Ashland, Missouri, was quiet and peaceful. The same could not be said for other places across the world. War was already breaking out in the Balkans, a precursor to World War I. Neither the decaying Ottoman Empire in Turkey nor the rigid ancient regime in Austria-Hungary could deal with the nationalistic fervor of Serbia and other ethnic groups in the region. It would continue to simmer until the assassination of the Archduke Ferdinand of Austria in the streets of Sarajevo in 1914 brought world war.

In Russia and Japan, changes in governments were determining the future courses for both countries. The instability of government of Tsar Nicholas II would prove ripe for revolution in Russia. The conflict in the Balkans would be the catalyst to topple the Tsar and bring Vladimir Lenin and his Bolshevik party into absolute power. In Japan, Emperor Meiji died, and the new emperor, Taisho, was significantly weaker than his father. Taisho was kept out of the public eye due to a number of physical infirmities. He was easily manipulated by many in his own government. His son and successor, the Emperor Hirohito would be unable to corral that government and years later Hirohito would preside as Japan was plunged into the Second World War.

The world though did know one bit of tranquility that year, when the world's best athletes gathered in Stockholm, Sweden for the Olympic Games. The Stockholm games were a model of peace and brotherhood. Jim Thorpe was the American star, taking the gold medals in the pentathlon and decathlon. The Swedish king, upon awarding him the second gold, declared, "you sir, are the greatest athlete in the world. "

But the biggest news of 1912 may have had to do with the unthinkable—the sinking of the unsinkable. In April the R.M.S. Titanic hit an iceberg and sank in the frigid waters of the North Atlantic. The Titanic was the finest ocean liner in the world, and the best way to travel the world knew. She sat sail from England bound for New York on her maiden voyage with a full crew and complement of passengers, including some of the wealthiest people in both London and New York City. When the Titanic went down she claimed over 1,500 lives.

Closer to home, the Missouri football Tigers were in the midst of a successful season of five wins and three losses. The Missouri State Fair in Sedalia celebrated its tenth year that summer.

As James and Margaret Glascock sat down with their family on the September day, what would they have thought about their world? What was of a concern to them? What did they even know about and care about?

News travelled only in two ways to Southern Boone County in those days. Newspapers and periodicals were the best source of news, while word of mouth was the surest. But they had no internet, no television, and even radio was nearly a decade in the future.

Following the St. Louis Cardinals, today a popular and often daily exercise for many of us, would have meant reading the paper to catch up on how they were doing. There was no other way. Had they decided to go see them in person, it would have meant catching the train to St. Louis, staying overnight in a nearby hotel, going to Robison's Field for the game, staying over in St. Louis another night before catching the train back to Columbia or Jeff City, and then riding back home to Wilton. Of course, for rural farm families in Missouri at the time, this trip would have been a big and expensive event. The newspaper *The University Missourian* advertised round trip tickets to St. Louis for only $5.85, which would have seemed a fortune to rural farm families of the day.

When the family sat down to dinner on that September day they could have talked about the sinking of the Titanic, the current presidential campaign, and even how perhaps how the Cardinals or the football Tigers were doing. Perhaps they talked about the upcoming State Fair, over in Sedalia. The fair was due to open that next weekend for seven big days! More likely though, they talked about their lives and what was going on around their circle of friends and family. How are the crops or the livestock doing? 1912 had been a very good year for agriculture in the Midwest. Would this winter be as harsh as the last? What was happening up at the church? All the talk probably centered around what was going on around them, while Grandpa Jimmy and Grandma Maggie bounced their first grandchild on their knee that year.

Much of what was going on in the world that year was, at the moment, of little consequence to them. But the world was beginning to change rapidly, and in their lifetimes they would experience many things that they could not have imagined on that September day.

What they did on that day continues. The gathering of their family has now reached its 100 year anniversary. That is what this book celebrates.

CHAPTER TWO

Just who were Grandpa Jimmy & Grandma Maggie?

So, just who were James Edmund Glascock and Margaret Ellen Rippeto? They were always called "Grandpa Jimmy" and "Grandma Maggie" by those in the family who can remember them.

 James Edmund Glascock was born on December 7, 1867, along with his twin sister, Emma Eliza. They were the ninth and tenth children of Franklin Ewing Glascock and Lucy Mustain Glascock (they would have a total of fourteen children, of which eight lived old enough to be married.) Franklin and Lucy were from Tennessee originally, before ending up in Missouri with a brief stop in northwest Arkansas. Franklin and Lucy had moved before the Civil War to the area near where the battle of Pea Ridge would take place in Arkansas. Lucy's parents and Franklin's brother also moved to the area. The Glascock and Mustain properties in Arkansas lay about half way between Bentonville, Arkansas, and Elkhorn Tavern (Elkhorn Tavern was a key location in the Battle of Pea Ridge.)

While the war raged around them (and Franklin sometimes joined in the fighting) Lucy's father, a minister, was called to a church near Ashland, Missouri. The Mustain and Glascock families packed up everything they had and moved en masse, buying land near Wilton, Missouri. James lived his entire life in the Wilton and Ashland areas. He joined the Goshen Primitive Baptist Church near Wilton, and remained a life-long member.

 Margaret Ellen Rippeto was born December 8, 1868, just a year and a day later than Grandpa Jimmy. She was the tenth of twelve children born to John and Matilda Jane Rippeto. The Rippeto family was originally from Virginia, and fought in the Revolutionary War. John was one of two brothers who eventually moved on to Missouri. Matilda Jane's family, the Sapps, were originally from Delaware, moving to Kentucky, and then on to Pike County, Missouri. In 1825, the family moved again, and finally settled in the Ashland area. She also joined Goshen Church in 1895.

There remains a bit of a mystery as to the exact spelling of Margaret's first name. Several sources, such as her tombstone, list it as "Margaret." Yet other documents spell her name as "Margret"—without the intervening "a". Which was it? We'll probably never know exactly how her parents intended that it be spelled, but for this story we'll go with her tombstone and the spelling that is memorialized in stone.

James and Margaret were married on November 10th of 1886 in Grandma Maggie's parent's home just up the road from James parent's home in Wilton. They both only seventeen at the time, which ended up making for a bit of a problem! James had to make two trips on horseback from Wilton to Columbia to get the marriage license. It seems that on the first trip (on November 9th) he had forgotten to take their parent's consent and had to return home to get it. He made the second trip the next day (the 10th) and returned just in time for the 4:00 p.m. wedding.

Perhaps it was fitting that Grandpa Jimmy just barely got there, as he was known for rarely being on time. He was often late to dinner, late to supper, and was never in a hurry to get anywhere—even church! He would get dressed and then disappear, usually out to the barn.

Grandma Maggie, on the other hand, was a stickler for timeliness. Dinner was at 12:00 noon sharp and she expected everyone to be at the table, ready to eat. Grandpa Jimmy of course was rarely there at noon. More than likely he would come wandering in about one o'clock. Grandma Maggie would fuss at him, telling him his dinner was now cold, but he paid little attention. Typically he'd grin and giggle, sit down and eat with no complaints.

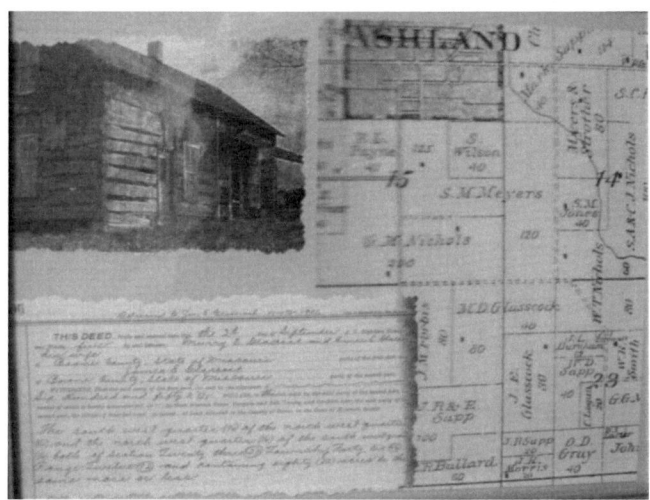 

Grandpa Jimmy had no complaints about the food as Grandma Maggie was a fine cook. Some of their grandkids walked by their house on the way home from school, and that meant a daily stop to see what Grandma would have for them. It might be cookies or a cold biscuit (which were reputed to be "the best ever eaten") that she had saved back from dinner. On the table was a square crystal bowl with a lid that Grandma Maggie kept filled with peach preserves. They went right along just fine with the biscuits.

One thing that Grandma Maggie simply couldn't stand though was to have flies in her house. She spent hours chasing and swatting them. Of course, since this was long before air conditioning and houses were kept cool by keeping the windows wide open, this meant she had flies to battle on a continual basis! But Grandma Maggie was persistent in her never-ending war against house flies.

For those who knew Grandpa Jimmy and Grandma Maggie, it seems that they would always describe them as having "strong" personalities. Actually, for the both of them, there was their way and the wrong way, which generally entailed everyone else's way! Grandpa Jimmy was stubborn and perhaps a bit bull-headed to be sure. He did however meet his match, and then some, in Grandma Maggie.

Typical of the way Grandpa Jimmy was is told in the story of Ross's move to Ashland to become the postmaster. After Grandma Maggie died, Grandpa Jimmy lived with some of his children, and at this time he was living with Ross and Lola. Ross announced that he was taking the job of postmaster in Hartsburg. Grandpa Jimmy was dead set against it and let his feelings be known. And not just once either—continually! To him this was the worst possible thing Ross could do and he said so time and time again. He was insistent that Ross and Lola needed to stay on the farm and they would continue farming together. Finally though, Ross had enough, and took his father to task about it, telling him it was his decision and it was the right decision for his family, and that Grandpa Jimmy was free to move with them or make other living arrangements. When Ross put his foot down, the discussion was over, and Grandpa Jimmy let it be. It seemed that he would argue and argue as long as it seemed he might prevail with his way. But once it was clear he would not, it was over and he held his peace.

Christmas was always a special time at Grandpa Jimmy's and Grandma Maggie's. Many family traditions came from those Christmas dinners. The women of the family would split into two groups—one group prepared the meal while the other group went into the room with the tree and decorated. The men and all the children were strictly forbidden from either place.

Dinner came first, usually a ham with all the trimmings. One of the most anticipated dishes was the fruit salad. The recipe was simple: every family brought a fruit and all of them were cut up and mixed together. So the long-anticipated fruit salad was never the same from year to year! Yet it was also one of the few times during the year that the family would have fruit, and that made the fruit salad a Christmas treat, something to anticipate and enjoy.

When dinner was finished, and the dishes were done, it was then time to open the doors to the Christmas tree and everyone go in. The grandkids in elementary school were expected to put on a "program" which generally consisted of whatever songs and program they were doing in school that year. Songs, skits, and speeches followed. Everyone joined in singing Christmas carols, and finally a prayer was offered. Then came the presents!

The family drew names every year. Gifts were distributed to everyone in the room, but no one opened theirs until all the presents had been distributed. Then the youngest would open their present, and this continued to the next-oldest, and then the next-oldest, until finally the oldest member of the family had opened his or hers. Everyone would show off their present and everyone got to see what everyone else had received.

If anyone knew Grandpa Jimmy at all, they knew he chewed tobacco constantly. And he could spit his "chew" quite a distance! The problem was, he couldn't hit any target and it went everywhere. During the time he lived with Ross and Lola, he had a pot near the stove to spit into. If he felt like it, he would, even from across the room, spit towards the pot. He rarely hit it. Instead, chew was all over the floor, on the wall, and on the stove. He wasn't concerned about it at all. But Lola, who could also let her feelings be known, constantly was complaining about the mess that she had to clean up.

When Grandpa Jimmy rode with the family to church on Sunday, he sat in the front seat, window down, so he could chew and spit as they travelled. The girls—Helen, Ola Mae, and Betty Jane—scrambled every week to not end right behind him and have to endure the spray every time he spit.

But the funniest story about Grandpa Jimmy and his chew has to be the time he was riding in the back seat while Esther Wren was driving. At some point, Jimmy opened the back door <u>while the car was travelling down the road</u> in order to properly spit. Esther, who is not as vocal as many in the family, jerked the car to a stop. She got out, stomped around to his door, pulled the door open, and began to berate her Grandpa about what he had done! Grandpa Jimmy quietly listened. Esther finished, slammed the door shut, and got back in. She pulled away, and never again did Grandpa Jimmy open the door while she was driving!

Grandpa Jimmy also dabbled in politics. He ran for county commissioner in 1932, losing in the Democratic primary in August.

Jimmy and Maggie enjoyed long lives together which culminated in their Golden Wedding Anniversary in 1936. A large number of family and friends stopped by their home on November 10, 1936, including several people who had also attended their wedding. They received gifts and baskets of food from the many well-wishers who shared the day with them. Their children presented a watch to their father and a new dress to their mother. The grandchildren gave Grandpa Jimmy a watch chain, and gave Grandma Maggie a necklace.

In the spring of 1941, Margaret Ellen, "Grandma Maggie," passed away on March 17th, at 72 years of age. She was laid to rest in the cemetery at Goshen Primitive Baptist Church in Wilton. On the occasion of her death, her youngest daughter, Chloe, wrote this poem:

Home is so lone, since mother's not here

Dark is her room and vacant her chair

Angels have taken her out of our care,

Still we recall our mother's sweet prayer.

Sleep mother sleep your troubles are o'er

Sweet bee the rest, you have needed before;

We all loved you, but God loved you more,

For he called you to that happy shore.

We buried you under the cedars

With heads bowed low we walked away.

God needed her to sing in heaven,

We'll meet again on that bright day.

Grandpa Jimmy remained in good health and had several years still ahead of him. He lived with Ross and Lola, and then with Oren and Clarice during those years. During World War II, Grandpa Jimmy always listened to the radio in the evenings to hear the daily war news. Since no one had electricity yet, that meant the radio was battery powered, and Grandpa Jimmy was a stickler that the batteries not become run down for when he wanted to listen. That often meant that his grandchildren were at odds with him, as they usually wanted to listen to music and even dance. But that was not "correct" according to Grandpa Jimmy, and he rarely relented and allowed it!

Oleta Wren Forsee recalls how Grandpa Jimmy and his buddy, Hale Mustain, spent a lot of time together during those years. He would often come into the house to tell his daughter, Clarice, that he and Hal were headed to Ashland, and asked if she needed anything. She would fuss at him and say, "Papa you need to change clothes, those are dirty." And Grandpa Jimmy would reply, "Oh these clothes are fine. I'm not dirty!" You can guess as how often he changed clothes to run up to Ashland.

In 1949, when the "birthday dinner" officially became the "family reunion" Grandpa Jimmy was named the "honorary president" of the reunion. Grandpa Jimmy became somewhat of a semi-invalid during the last two or three years of his life. This placed a bit of a burden on Oren and Clarice as someone needed to stay with him even during big family events.

James Edmund, "Grandpa Jimmy," died from pneumonia on January 15, 1953, at the age of 85 years, 1 month, and 8 days old, at the home of Oren and Clarice. He also laid to rest at Goshen, besides Grandma Maggie, his partner in this life.

1915

CHAPTER THREE:

How Did We Get Here?

How did the Glascock family end up in Boone County?

Three brothers from England—Thomas, Richard, and Robert Glascock—left their parents, Henery and Marjory, and sailed for Virginia in 1643 A.D. Thomas and his wife Jane made their home along the James River in Virginia. They had three sons, Gregory, Thomas, and John.

Gregory married Mary Fauntleroy and had a son, Thomas, and twin girls, Mary and Anne. Thomas married Sarah Stone and had six children. Their youngest son, Peter, married Jane Fishback and they had nine children. Among their children was Peter Glascock, Jr. The family remained in Virginia all through this time.

Peter, Jr. married Elizabeth Madden and they had eight children. Peter and Elizabeth moved their family to Tennessee. One son, George Washington Glascock married Elizabeth Graham. They would have a very large family of ten children. They were: Peter Murry, Richard, Elizabeth, Charnel, Catherine (Kate), Henry (Dee), Rosannah, George Washington, Jr., Jane, and finally Franklin Ewing. Franklin Ewing, the father of Grandpa Jimmy, was born June 22, 1826, in Williamson County, Tennessee.

Franklin grew up on the family farm and never received any formal education. Throughout his life, he never could really read or write. In 1850 he met and married Lucy Breint Mustain. Lucy was the daughter of Shadrick and Margaret Mustain. She was born on the 16th of October, 1833. She was only 16 years old when she married Franklin. The 1850 census shows them still living in Marshall County, Tennessee.

About the year 1856, Franklin and Lucy decided to move west. Franklin's brother, George, Jr., decided to move with them as well. Franklin and Lucy used oxen to pull their wagon, while George and his wife (also named Lucy) used horses. The oxen had

significantly more endurance. Franklin and Lucy ended near Bentonville, in northwest Arkansas. His brother went a bit further to the north and settled in Lawrence County in Missouri. They settled in and soon had three children—Murry, Elizabeth (called Betty), and Margaret Jane (Janie). They moved near the head of Bushy Creek on Little Sugar Creek Road, near some small mountains. One of those mountains was known as Pea Ridge—soon to become famous.

The outbreak of the Civil War radically changed the lives of Franklin, Lucy and their family. They sold part of their farm in April of 1861, seemingly in preparation to move should it become necessary. They sold the remainer of the farm in January of 1862, and moved in with some of Lucy's family living nearby.

The war came very close to home in March of 1862 when the Union army of General Samuel Curtis clashed with Confederate forced under General Earl Van Dorn. Curtis had pushed into Arkansas and fortified some of the heights of Pea Ridge. Van Dorn army though became split, with one wing, under Benjamin McCullough, pushing east around the mountain. The other wing, under Missourian Sterling Price, ended up going to the west of Pea Ridge and arriving at the battle field a day later than McCullough. McCullough was killed, and though the Union army suffered severe casualties, it was the Confederates who retired from the field.

Did Franklin Ewing Glascock fight at the Battle of Pea Ridge? Little is really known about his service in the Confederate army. The only record of any service comes at the Battle of Prairie Grove, also in Arkansas. There he was listed as a soldier in Elliot's Missouri Cavalry, as part of Jo Shelby's Raiders. Elliot's Missouri Calvary shows up in the Confederate Order of Battle as part of Shelby's "Iron Brigade" at several battles across Missouri and Arkansas.

It seems quite possible that Franklin joined in with the forces of Major General Sterling Price at Pea Ridge. The battle was quite close to where his family lived, and it seems likely that he joined in whether or not he was actually inducted into the Confederate Army at the time. Elliot's Cavalry was an irregular unit, meaning that the soldiers probably came and went as they chose. When there was a battle looming, they showed up. When things were quiet, they slipped away home. The roster of Elliot's Missouri Cavalry lists no unit designation for Franklin, though he was on the roster. Interestingly enough, the men who primarily made up Elliot's Cavalry were from twelve Missouri counties that included Boone, Callaway, Randolph, Cooper, and Henry. Franklin found himself fighting alongside men from near his future home.

Franklin apparently had such admiration for General Price (as did most of the Missouri State Guards) that he named his fourth child for him, Sterling Price Glascock. This son was born in January of 1863, showing that Franklin had at least one opportunity to be away from the army in 1862.

Things were difficult for families in Northwest Arkansas, and Lucy and the children moved with her father and mother to Polk County, Missouri. Towards the end of the war, Shadrick Mustain, preacher, was called to a church along Spencer's Ford in Boone County, near the little town of Wilton. After the war, Franklin rejoined the family and they put down roots in Wilton.

Franklin and Lucy had seven more children born to them in Wilton. Julia Ann came along in 1866. Mary was born and died in 1869. Elvia was born in 1871 and died in 1875. George was born in 1873. Their youngest, Shannon, was born in 1878 and lived to be ten years old.

 In 1867, Franklin and Lucy welcomed twins into the world, a son, James Edmund and a daughter, Emma Elizabeth. James and Emma grew up in Wilton as the Glascock family put down deep roots into soil of Southern Boone County.

The Glascock name found itself attached to a mountain in Arkansas, and counties in Georgia and Texas. And perhaps most importantly to our family, the Glascock Branch is the name of the creek at the bottom of the hill from Goshen Church, where so many of the family were baptized.

This was now the home of Franklin and Lucy, and James Edmund Glascock would grow up among the hills and woods around Wilton. The deep roots they put down remain today.

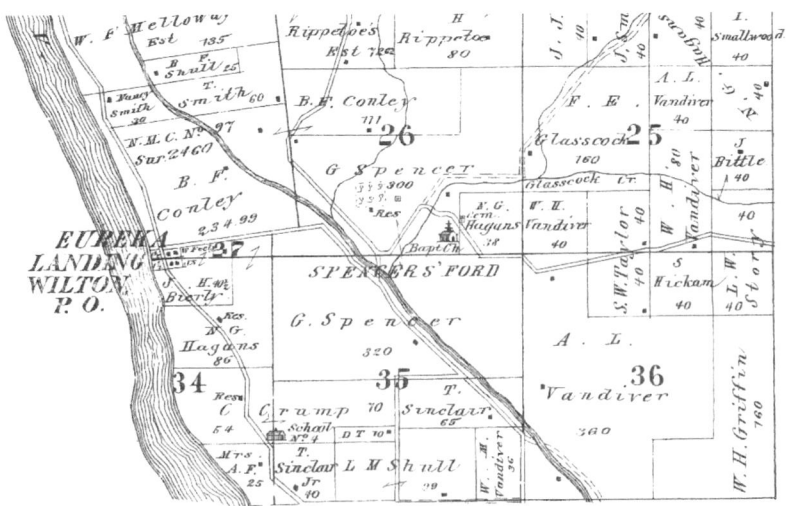

CHAPTER FOUR:

The First Birthday Dinner

The annual Glascock reunion met for the first time on Tuesday, September 24, 1912. No one is left who was there to tell us about the gathering, but we can have a pretty good idea as to how the day went. The later recollections of the reunion, which became the record of the reunion, tell that James and Margaret, along with Fred and Belle and their baby boy, Edmond, spent the day at John and Stella's to celebrate the birthdays of Fred and John. The official reunion records don't tell us anything about the younger children of James and Margaret's (Ross, Clarice, and Chloe.) Often times the earliest records of the reunion often did not list everyone who might actually have been in attendance. Some years they would state that everyone was there, and in others they simply said nothing as to who or how many were there.

The hand-written diary of Chloe though suggests that of the three only Ross may have be in attendance. Clarice and Chloe were said to have been at school during that day and thus missed the dinner. Ross, though of normal school age today, had already completed the eighth grade, the last year of school that he attended. Most likely this was the case. Family gatherings were important and a "big deal" to James and Margaret and all three still lived at home. There can be little doubt that the girls would not have been left at home for the day. Perhaps whoever wrote down the reunion record assumed that we would understand where the younger children were that day.

So we can be sure that the very first "birthday celebration" (as it was originally called) was attended by Grandpa Jimmy and Grandma Maggie, Fred and Belle and their baby boy, Edmond, the hosts, John and Stella, and possibly Ross.

There is another family member who also may have attended—Grandpa Jimmy's mother, Lucy Glascock. Nothing is said as to her being there, but her obituary in the Ashland Bugle (she died just over a year later on November 1, 1913) stated that she died at the home of her son, James E. Glascock. Earlier accounts indicate that in 1910 she moved in with her daughter, Elizabeth, and her son-in-law Orville Allison. Another account suggests that she bought a home in Wilton. When did she move in with James & Margaret? We simply don't know. Perhaps she was there on a trip, before becoming ill and dying in 1913. But whatever the case, it is possible that she was living with Jimmy and Maggie in 1912 and 1913 and may have been at these first birthday celebrations. But, we simply don't know for sure.

What was the day like? The day before the birthday celebration had seen a high temperature of about 75, while the overnight low was in the low 50's. The University Missourian newspaper forecast that the high temperature for the 24th would be in the low 70's, but rain would be moving in that evening, with brisk winds to start a cooling trend that week. A strong storm system from out of the Texas panhandle was headed into

Missouri. But the morning and afternoon would be a beautiful and pleasant autumn day. The forecast proved correct about the pleasant temperatures, but the rain that evening was spotty and amounted to only a few hundredths.

What was the dinner like? Again, we have no one left to tell us precisely, but we do have plenty of family members who attended family dinners for many years, both for the birthday celebrations and for other occasions. Dinners at family gatherings were exactly what one would expect rural farm families to have in those days. There were no trips to the store, so anything they had was something that they either grew themselves, or they could trade for from a neighbor perhaps. The main meat course was most likely pork. Pork was the major source of meat on small family farms at that time. Beef required much more land than pigs, making it more expensive to raise. To buy a side of beef would have been quite expensive as well and was really out of the question. Besides the cost, there were issues with how to keep the meat from spoiling without the refrigeration we depend upon today.

Chicken was also a possibility for the main course, as chickens were also an economical product for most small farmers. But given the memories of those who attended family dinners in the 1930's, boiled ham seemed to be a typical dinner main course, and was probably what was on the table at that first birthday celebration.

The meat would have been served with potatoes and other vegetables on the table as well. Potatoes would have been either mashed with gravy or might have been served boiled. Green beans, sweet potatoes, turnips and even field corn could have made up the rest of the meal. Many vegetables that we night normally have a 100 years later would not have been on that table that day. While we might, for instance, have a taste for a nice tossed lettuce salad, lettuce would have been highly seasonal and unavailable at the end of a long, hot summer. Most likely, it was rarely grown.

Pies would have most likely been the dessert for the day. They didn't require refrigeration and could be done ahead of time. Fruit pies, such as apple, or cobblers, such as peach, would likely have been the final course for that big family meal.

When it was dinner time, the family would have gathered at the table to sit together and eat. A prayer for blessing the meal and the family would have been said, and the meal began. Everyone was expected to be in their place for dinner.

That dinner on that beautiful autumn day began the tradition we continue with the Glascock family reunion. Perhaps the most important discussion that September day was to make this an annual dinner. That began our tradition.

CHAPTER FIVE:

Birthday Dinners and Reunions Through The Years

At the first birthday dinner in 1912 the decision was made to make it an annual event, to be held on the fourth Sunday of the month of September. The dinner would rotate between the homes of James and Margaret, Fred and Belle, and John and Stella. The first dinner, in 1912, was at the home of John and Stella. In 1913 James and Margaret hosted.

Several family members, Clarice and Chloe in particular, were not at the dinner in 1912. But the records show that for many years after that, every member of the family attended. And so it was in 1913. However, grief did cast a shadow on the gathering that year, as the first child of John and Stella, a daughter, was stillborn that year.

In 1914, there was no dinner. Little is said in the records about why, except that Stella was unable to attend. This may have been the determining factor in cancelling the dinner. It would be the first of only two cancellations in the 100 years since 1912.

The dinner was held again in 1915 at Fred and Belle's with everyone in attendance. This was the case for the next two years.

In 1918, Ross was away in the U.S. Army. Then again in 1919 everyone attended. This began a streak of "perfect attendance" that continued in the 1930's.

The 1919 reunion featured two new members. Oren Wren joined the family when he married Clarice. Fred and Belle added a baby daughter when Alice Elizabeth was born that July. For the next dozen years there was at least one new member of the family to celebrate.

Throughout the 1920's the dinner continued to rotate between the three homes, and every year everyone came and at least one new member joined the family.

The dinner in 1931 marked the first time in a dozen years that no new members were present. In 1936, the streak of "perfect attendance" also came to an end, as heavy rains that month made it impossible for all to attend. Jack and Erma, along with their baby, Italene, were unable to attend.

In 1937 the dinner enjoyed a temporary expansion when the relatives and friends of Lafayette Rippeto were invited as he was visiting from California. (Grandma Maggie was from the Rippeto family.) Around 130 people attended, shattering any previous record for attendance!

Since the 1913 dinner the family had enjoyed nothing but growth and celebration. The death of Ross and Lola's oldest girl, Pid, brought that to a temporary halt in 1939. This marked only the second loss in the family over the past 27 years. Unfortunately the third loss followed in 1940, when the infant daughter of Dorothy and Wayne died that year.

The 1941 dinner featured yet another loss. This time however, it was not one of the younger members, but rather Grandma Maggie.

With the outbreak of the Second World War, more and more family members were unable to attend as so many of family's young men were overseas serving their country. Eight members were missing in 1943. With this, the dinner in 1944 became only the second reunion to be cancelled in the 100 years since 1912. Many of the boys were away overseas, and their families also often were not able to attend. Lola Glascock was also hospitalized at the time, and it seemed prudent to cancel the dinner.

In 1945 the reunion was held again, though attendance remained low. The cause this year was due to the heavy September rains that made getting to John and Stella's home impossible. The dinner was switched to Dorothy's home (their daughter) and only a few attended.

The reunion though rebounded in 1946. There were 55 living members of the family, and most were there. The reunion was also held early in September, on the 1st, as both

Juno and Bobbie were home on leave at the same time. By now the family was growing with new marriages and new children every year.

By 1949, the dinner was becoming too large to manage without some structure. Ross suggested that the family organize the dinner by electing offices every year to serve through the next reunion. Further, the "Birthday Dinner" was renamed "The Family Reunion." A collection of 25 cents per family was adopted, to pay for paper plates and cups, and any other needed items. Jack Glascock was elected as President. Dorothy Gilpin served as vice-president. Helen Smith was elected as Secretary-Treasurer. Finally, Grandpa Jimmy, as the oldest living member of the family, was made "Honorary President" and "Head" of the family.

The next year, in 1950, the family met at Oren and Clarice's to accommodate Grandpa Jimmy, who was confined to his bed. 69 of the 70 members were present, with Juno being overseas in the military. Ross opened the business meeting with prayer. Dorothy moved up from the vice-president to president. Virgil Wren was elected president and Helen was re-elected at Secretary-Treasurer for the first of many times. The reunion closed with everyone signing "God Be With You."

The 1953 reunion was hosted by Ross and Lola at the Hartsburg American Legion dining hall. This marked the first time that the reunion was not actually held at a home. It also marked the first reunion since the death of Grandpa Jimmy, who had passed away earlier that year in January. The reunion was now 43 years old, and this marked only the fifth loss in those years. Fred Glascock was made the "Honorary President" as the oldest living member of the family. The family now numbered 75 living members.

In 1958 the reunion was held at the home of Ed and Betty Blythe in Jefferson City. This marked the only time the reunion was ever held outside of Boone County.

1960 marked the death of the reunion's second Honorary President, Fred Wilbur Glascock, in July of that year. His brother, John, became the next Honorary President. The 1961 reunion came on John's birthday, September 24th, exactly 49 years to the day of the first birthday dinner.

In 1962, the reunion began work on a family history to commemorate the first fifty years of the reunion. While the offices of President and Vice President changed yearly, the reunion did express its grateful thanks to Helen Smith who continued to serve every year as the Secretary-Treasurer of the reunion. She had not sought the post, but never complained and always faithfully discharged her duties.

In 1963 the reunion moved the Home Arts Building in Columbia, on Clinkscales Street. It would remain there for several years. A discussion had been held for the past couple of reunions about moving it earlier in month, in an effort to accommodate those who did not live in Central Missouri. It was decided at this time to keep the reunion on the fourth Sunday in September.

In 1964 the family grew to have 125 members. They also decided to make the minutes available in written form. This cost each family an additional 50 cents.

A new committee was appointed in 1965 to work on the family history. It consisted of John Glascock, Clarice Wren, Chloe Calvin, and Belle Glascock (Fred's wife.) The intent was to publish a book by the next reunion. They did indeed have a family history book ready by the 1966 reunion. The cost of printing and the binders for the books cost just over $2.00. They had 50 copies printed. The books were sold for $2.50 with the balance from the books going in the treasury. Also the family contribution was increased from 25 cents to 50 cents due to the increased cost of renting a hall. This reunion also marked the first time it was held in the Ashland American Legion hall. It also marked the loss of the third Honorary President, when John died in July of that year. Ross became the new Honorary President, following his dad and brothers into the position.

Ross died in April of 1970, and with his death, the title of Honorary President passed to Clarice Wren, his sister. The family continued to grow throughout the decade of the

1970's. The reunion continued to be held at the American Legion Hall in Ashland into the 1980's and 1990's. Chloe passed away in 1980, the only one of the children of Jimmy and Maggie to not hold the position of Honorary President.

1979 would also mark the end of her long term as Secretary-Treasurer for Helen Smith. After those many years of service, it was decided to share that load among others in the family.

In 1985 the reunion decided to update the family history from the 1967 version. A supplement to that history was to be made available.

The reunion now regularly attracted over 100 people every year. In 1987 the family altered the election of officers to coincide with the upcoming family hosting future reunions. The Vice-President would be elected from the family scheduled to host the reunion two years in the future. The Vice-President would then move up as President when his or her family would host the next year.

In 1988 the supplement to the 1967 family history was again taken up. Jerry and Linda Arnold agreed to spearhead the effort. The reunion sent a letter of recognition and thanks to them for their help. A special collection was also taken up that year for Clarice Wren, the current Honorary President. She was thus also made the family's Honorary Historian.

Clarice Wren died two days before the 1989 reunion, the 77th anniversary of the first birthday dinner. This marked the last of Grandpa Jimmy's and Grandma Maggie's children to pass away from among us. For the first time, the position of Honorary President was not filled. However the position of Honorary Historian was passed onto Lola Glascock.

1992 marked the first time since 1965 that the reunion was not held in the American Legion hall in Ashland. Instead, it was held in the Masonic Hall just down the street. Attendance had declined, and was now numbering around 60 to 80 people every year. The supplement to the family history was also available for the first time. It had been compiled by Jerry and Linda Arnold. The reunion honored them with a gift certificate for their hard work. 1992 also marked the return of Helen Smith to the position of Secretary-Treasurer for one more year.

The reunion lasted only the one year in the Masonic Hall. In 1993 it moved to its current location, the Optimist Building in Ashland. This allowed for more room and perhaps most importantly, room for the children to play. After several years of having everyone bring their own table service, it was also decided to provide plates, cups, plastic-ware, and napkins for the next year. The move to the Optimist Building was a great success, and the reunion continues to meet there to this day. By 1994, attendance was back up to well over 120 people.

T-shirts were made available in 1994, with each branch of the family having a different color. Attendance for the 1995 reunion went over 140 people, as enthusiasm for the reunion continued to build again.

By the year 2000, thoughts begin to turn to the coming 100th anniversary, slated for 2012. Several members got together to begin the process. They included Ola Mae Taggart (from the Ross line), Lora Jones (from the Clarice line), Esther Wren (from the Clarice line), Marilyn Bennett (from the Chloe line), and Oleta and Joe Forsee (from the Clarice line.)

In 2007, Noel Blythe, a grandson of Ross, agreed to write the family history. Reunions over the next few years included a plea for information and stories about the reunion and the family. A committee was organized that consisted of Noel, Ola Mae, Lora, Esther, Marilyn, Alberta Gilpin (from the John line), Pam Slama (from the Fred line), and Nancy Bryant (also from the Fred line.) To this group fell the task of writing a new family history and organizing the celebration for the 100th anniversary reunion.

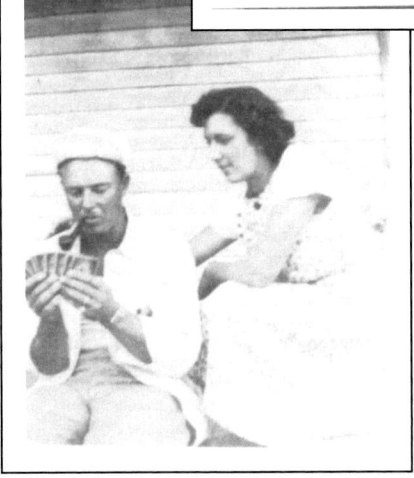

CHAPTER SIX:

The 100th Anniversary Reunion

The culmination of this 100th anniversary reunion came on the weekend of September 22nd and 23rd in 2012. The reunion was held at the Optimist Building in Ashland. An open house was held on Saturday, the 22nd, to afford family members and friends the chance to gather, enjoy punch and cookies, and look at the displays gathered for the reunion. Nearly a hundred friends and family members turned out on Saturday.

The committee created several displays for the reunion, including several picture collages. The one generating the most interest was this collage of every person from the family who had served in armed services.

Additional collages included photos from a wide spectrum of family members from across many years:

A cake celebrating the occasion was displayed setting on a cake plate that originally belonged to Grandma Maggie, and now belonged to Marilyn Bennett.

The most prominent display was a collection of quilts done by members of the family. These included quilts from Grandma Maggie Glascock, Stella Glascock, Belle Glascock, Lola Glascock, Clarice Wren, and Chloe Calvin. Each was done in the particular style of each of these early matriarchs of the family. The quilt from Grandma Maggie was of particular interest and had been passed on down to her youngest daughter Chloe, and then to her youngest daughter Marilyn.

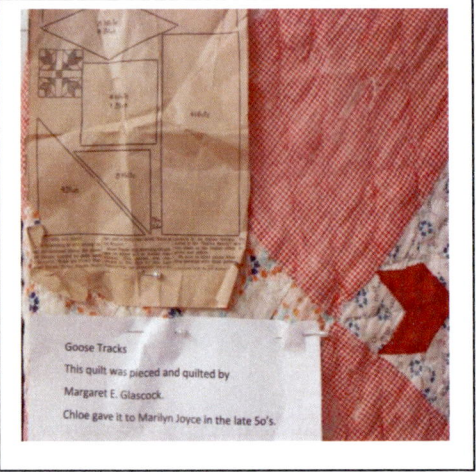

Goose Tracks
This quilt was pieced and quilted by
Margaret E. Glascock.
Chloe gave it to Marilyn Joyce in the late 50's.

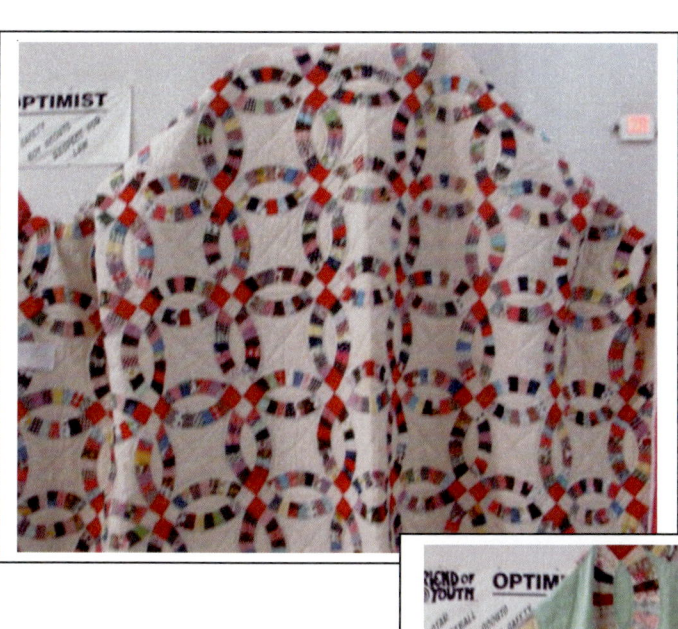

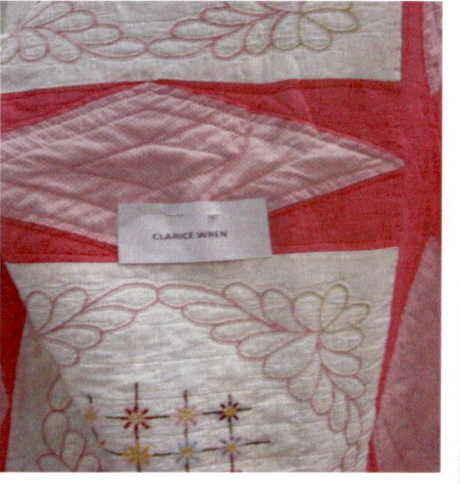

 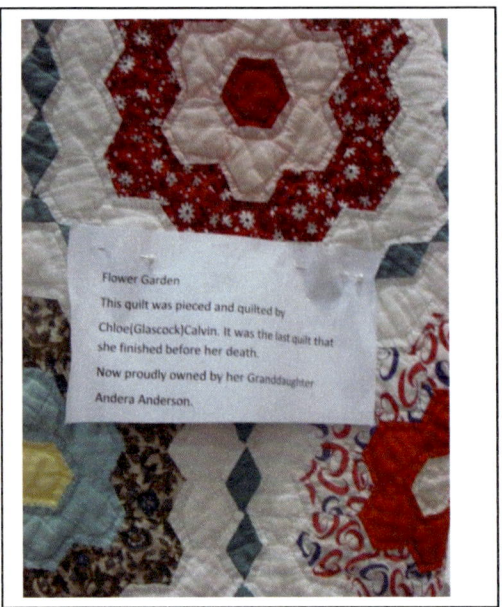

Flower Garden

This quilt was pieced and quilted by Chloe(Glascock)Calvin. It was the last quilt that she finished before her death.

Now proudly owned by her Granddaughter Andera Anderson.

A book of family charts was also available for corrections and updates, so that we can have and maintain these records for the future.

The official count of those in attendance for the reunion on Sunday came to 233 family members and guests. Twenty-seven members of the Fred and Belle line attended. The single remaining blood descendant of John and Stella's line (Alberta Gilpin) was there, along with eleven members of her adopted family. Seventy-nine members of Ross and Lola's family attended, along with 3 guests. Clarice and Oren's family was the largest at the reunion, eighty-two members and one guest strong. Thirty-one members of Chloe and Cloid's family were there to represent that line of the family.

Pictures were taken in abundance. Joe Forsee served as the "official" photographer. Photographs of each family were taken as we got in line to eat, along with hundreds of other pictures taken by dozens of people.

Descendents of Fred & Belle Glascock

Descendents of John & Stella Glascock

Descendents of Ross & Lola Glascock

Descendents of Clarice & Oren Wren

Descendents of Chloe & Cloid Calvin

The nine living granddaughters of Grandpa Jimmy and Grandma Maggie all attended the reunion. They were (L to R): (seated) Ola Mae Taggart, Helen Smith, Esther Lewis, (standing) Betty Jane Blythe, Maggie Lu Crane, Marilyn Bennett, Emma Fern McDonald, Lora Ann Jones, Oleta Forsee.

The oldest living descendent in the family was Esther Wren Lewis, who was born on May 20th, in 1920. The youngest living descendent was Elysie Gregori, born on August 20th of 2012, attending her first reunion at the age of 1 month and 4 days. Esther is the great-great-great-aunt of Elysie.

The kids were able to enjoy a nice fall afternoon outside as Clay Austin provides a hayride around the grounds of the Optimist Building.

Vincent Calvin served as president of the reunion, as it was the Chloe and Cloid family's turn to host the reunion. Nancy Bryant was vice-president and Brenda Austin served as Secretary-Treasurer. Nancy ascended to president as the Fred and Belle line would host in 2013. Rex Taggart accepted the position of Vice-President, and Brenda Austin was retained for the Secretary-Treasurer position.

At the business meeting for the reunion, Noel Blythe suggested that the family re-institute the position of "Honorary President" of the family. This position had been filled by the oldest living descendent of Grandpa Jimmy and Grandma Maggie and had been unfilled since the death Clarice Wren. Brenda Austin made the motion and Noel seconded it. The motion carried on a voice vote, and the oldest living member of the family, Esther Lewis, was made the Honorary President of the Glascock family.

The reunion committee also had proposed a service project for the 100th Anniversary Reunion. A collection was taken before and during the reunion to donate to the maintenance of Goshen Cemetery where so many family members have been laid to rest. A total of $1,130 was donated as of the reunion. This included $400 that was donated from the treasury of the reunion. This donation to the Goshen Cemetery was made in the name of James and Margaret Glascock.

Door prizes were also given out. Beverly Steelman, Kamdyn Craig, and Lindsay Campbell all won portraits of Grandpa Jimmy and Grandma Maggie and their family. Megan Craig and Chris Bowden won mums that were donated by Marilyn Bennett.

The committee for the 100th Anniversary Reunion consisted (from L to R): Esther Lewis (a daughter of Clarice), Marilyn Bennett (a daughter of Chloe), Lora Jones (a daughter of Clarice), Noel Blythe (chairman & a grandson of Ross), Nancy Bryant (a granddaughter of Fred), Alberta Gilpin (a granddaughter of John), Pam Slama (a granddaughter of Fred), and Ola Mae Taggart (a daughter of Ross).

PHOTOS FROM SATURDAY'S OPEN HOUSE, SEPTEMBER 22nd, 2012

PHOTOS FROM SUNDAY'S REUNION, SEPTEMBER 23rd, 2012

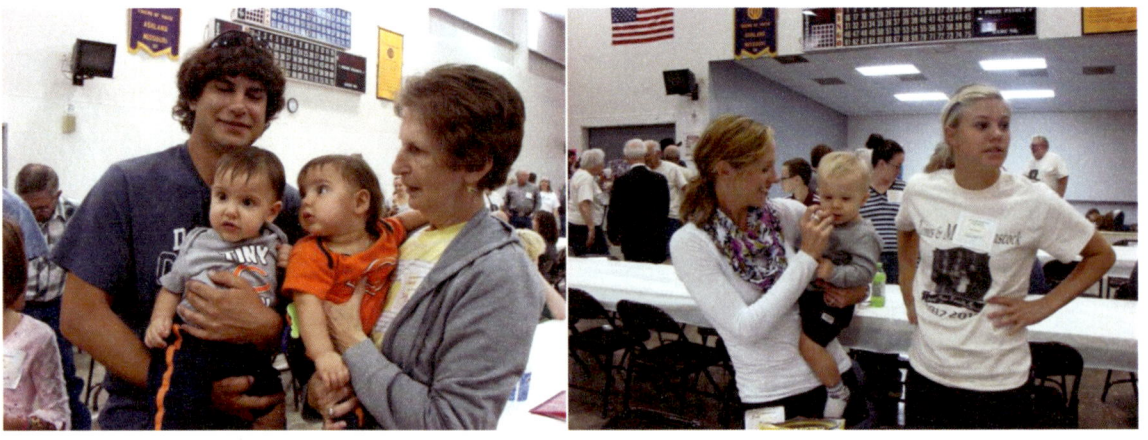

CHAPTER SEVEN:

The Family of Fred & Belle Glascock

James and Margaret began their family when their first child, a son, was born on September 26, 1887. They named him Fred Wilbur. The new family lived south of Ashland, along the current U.S. Highway 63 between Peterson Road and Forsee Road.

The world saw much change in 1887, though most of it would not have been noticeable to the farm families around Ashland and Wilton. It was the Golden Jubilee for Queen Victoria in Great Britain, marking her 50th year on the throne. The contact lens was invented that year. Sherlock Holmes made his first appearance in Sir Arthur Conan Doyle's *A Study in Scarlet*. And Punxsutawney, Pennsylvania celebrated "Groundhog Day" for the very first time. But not much of that would have meant very much to the Glascock family at the time.

Fred spent his entire childhood in the Ashland and Wilton areas. That area would pretty well have been Fred's entire world. Travel was prohibitively expensive for rural farm families during that time. A trip up to Columbia or down to Jefferson City would have been probable, but anything further might have been a "once-in-a-life-time" event. But Fred surely made the trip from his parent's home near Ashland to his grandparent's home (Franklin and Lucy) near Wilton many, many times in his young life.

Fred grew up familiar with life on the family farm. Chores had to be done, and he was sure to have done his share. The good, bountiful years brought a few extras. The lean years brought just enough to live on, and nothing more. Such was the life of family farms around the turn of the century.

Fred married Josie Belle Sapp on December 28, 1910. Josie Belle was the daughter of Charles and Alcie Jane Sapp. Her parents held an unusual distinction—both of them were born in the month of May, they were baptized in the month of May, they were married in the month of May, and finally they both died in the month of May.

Within the year, Fred and Belle started their family. A son, the first of seven children, was born to them on October 13th of 1911. They named him Edmund Leland, though they called him "Jack." Thus began a sort of "tradition" in Fred and Belle's family—no one seemed to go by their given name. Rather, Fred nicknamed all his children. In fact, Fred and Belle became known as "Daddy Fred" and "Momma Belle" to their children and grandchildren. Thus Edmund became "Jack."

A daughter, Alma Lorane, was born to Fred and Belle next, on the 27th of May in 1914. She became known as "Duke." Fred and Belle were living on what was known as the Ben Anderson farm in the Wilton Bottoms during the early years of their marriage. By the time the next child arrived they had moved to the Wilson's place, close to the farm of Fred's sister, Chloe, and her husband Cloid.

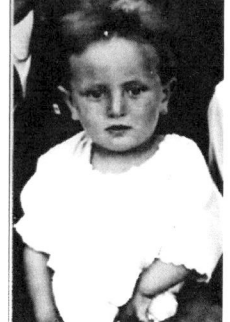

Another son, Estil Dudley Glascock, arrived on December 5, 1916. Estil, of course, was also nicknamed. He would always be known as "Pud."

In March of 1919 Fred and Belle bought a farm along with his father and his brother, Ross. The farm was located about a mile-and-a-half east of Wilton along Cedar Tree Lane. The farm surrounded Goshen church and the farm of James' father, Franklin. James and Margaret lived in the two story house on the farm. Fred and Belle moved their family into the house across the road, which was originally the house for the "hired hands." Ross and Lola moved into a house at the bottom of the hill of the farm.

In 1919 Daddy Fred and Momma Belle not only moved to the farm, but they also saw another increase in their young family. A second daughter, Alice Elizabeth Glascock, was born that July, on the 10th of the month. She would be nicknamed "Judy."

Over the next several years, their family added three more sons. Their third son was born in 1921. Fred Ewel Glascock arrived on August 29th of that year, and was nicknamed "Juno." A fourth son, Murry Elston Glascock, was born November 9th, 1925. He would be nicknamed "Mutt." Finally a seventh child and fifth son completed the family. Bobbie Elmore Glascock, called "Rube," was born on October 12th, in 1927.

 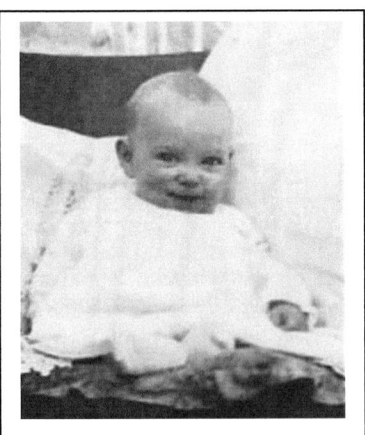 

The children all attended grade school in Wilton and the older ones went to high school in Ashland. They spent their summers leading the typical life of farm families during the 1920's and 1930's. Life on the farm during those times was difficult. The Great Depression for small farms began much earlier in rural America than across the rest of the country.

By the mid-1930's, Daddy Fred's and Momma Belle's family began to leave the nest and begin families of their own. Jack married Erma Stella Taylor on November 30, 1933. Judy (Alice Elizabeth) was married to Warren Woodson on the 9th of July in 1938. Lorane married Basey Vanlandingham on December 31st, the last day of 1940. Estil married Berniece Begemann on May 5th, 1941.

World War Two interrupted family plans a bit over the next few years. Estil left his new bride at home as he was inducted into the U.S. Army in January of 1942. Murry went into the U.S. Navy in 1944. The two younger brothers, Juno and Bobbie, both joined the army in 1946.

Family plans might have been interrupted a bit, but even the war could not completely bring those to a halt. Daddy Fred and Momma Belle already had several grandchildren by the outbreak of the war.

Italene Glascock, the daughter of Jack and Erma, was the first, making them grandparents on September 24th, 1934. A second granddaughter followed in 1940 when Jonna Belle Woodson was born to Judy and Warren on April 24th. Daddy Fred and Momma Belle welcomed their first grandson, as proud parents Judy and Warren added James Woodson, born March 14th of 1942. A second grandson, A. B. Vanlandingham, II, was born to Lorane and Basey on February 19th, of 1943.

Pud and Berniece added another grandson to Daddy Fred's and Momma Belle's family, when Jerome was born on May 11th, 1944. Jack and Erma added another granddaughter in 1945, when Martha Karen was born on the 25th of June in 1945. For the third year in a row, in 1946, Fred and Belle saw a new grandchild. Lorane and Basey added another grandson when Forrest Barry Vanlandingham was born on November 13th of 1945. The records of the reunion noted that in this year of 1946 that James and Margaret had their tenth great-grandchild. Seven of those were from Daddy Fred's and Momma Belle's family!

While the attention of the younger sons had been primarily focused on military service, the end of the war brought more additions to the family. Murry married Nancy Lee Woolery on the 6th of June in 1947. Bobbie married Bettie Sue Garrett on the 24th of May in 1949. Juno married Ella Mae Pace in 1951. With these new families beginning, more grandchildren were sure to be on the way!

Judy and Warren had their second daughter, Mariann Woodson, born in 1948. Ronald Murry Glascock was born on May 27th of 1948, to new parents Murry and Nancy. They added a second son in 1949 when Fred William Glascock was born on November 25th. Bobbie and Bettie Sue began their family with the birth of Bobbie Elmore Glascock, Jr. on April 3rd, 1950.

One of the biggest events in the life of Fred and Belle happened in 1950 when Fred was elected County Clerk for Boone County. They left the farm and moved to Columbia. They lived in a big white two story house on Route N. Fred would be re-elected as County Clerk twice. They eventually moved back to Ashland, in a white house out on Route M. Fred was the County Clerk for Boone County for ten years. For some of his grandchildren, he seemed very much at home among the books of records and deeds in the office.

The 1950's saw the family of Daddy Fred and Momma Belle continued to grow, and it seemed to be all girls! Juno married Ella Mae Pace in 1951. After that, the granddaughters began to arrive. Murry and Nancy welcomed Nancy Louise Glascock on December 15th of 1951. The year 1953 saw their family add three new girls! Juno and Ella Mae were blessed with the arrival of a daughter, Theresa Denise Glascock on the 13th of April. Bobbie and Bettie Sue added Pamela Lee Glascock to their family on June 30th. And Lorane and Basey completed their family with a daughter, Becky Lynn Vanlandingham, born on the 1st of August. Juno and Ella Mae added a second daughter the next year when Joella Fae Glascock was born on July the 17th, 1954. Judy and Warren's family expanded with first the arrival of Connie Jane Woodson on May 2nd, 1955 and then the birth of a fourth daughter, Sarah Jean Woodson, on May 10th, 1957. All-in-all, Daddy Fred and Momma Belle had added six granddaughters in a row.

The string of girls was broken by the birth John Duane Glascock to Bobbie and Bettie Sue, on May 6th, 1959. The family was nearly complete (at least as far as grandchildren.) Murry and Nancy added two more sons—James Edmund Glascock, born on June 22nd of 1962, and Herbert Scott Glascock, born on February 6th, 1965.

Sadly, Daddy Fred would not live to see these last two grandsons. In the summer of 1960 he fell ill, and died on July 11th. He was 73 years old.

Fred and Belle would have been married for fifty years in December of that year, falling less than six months short of that date. In a family where 50th anniversary celebrations have been common, they deserve recognition for coming so close. Only his untimely death prevented it.

Belle couldn't stay in the house where he died, and moved across the street. Belle stayed in the Ashland area, and lived for many more productive years. By the 1970's though, she could no longer stay by herself. The house was sold and she lived with both Pud and then with Lorane. She fell and broke her hip and had to be moved into a nursing home. She developed pneumonia and died shortly thereafter, on December 30th, 1977. She would see several of her grandchildren marry and start their own families and would enjoy several great-grandchildren before her death. Belle would be buried beside her husband Fred at Memorial Cemetery in Columbia.

In the end, Fred and Belle would have twenty grandchildren and many great-grandchildren. The family was quite large by this time, and when they gathered on important occasions, the family remembers that they were kind of split into the "town people" (the families of Jack, Lorane, and Judy) who lived in the Columbia area, and the "country folk" (the families of Pud, Murry, and Bobbie) who lived and farmed in Ashland and Wilton. The seventh child, Juno, was a career serviceman, and he and his family lived all across the globe. Yet on all the important occasions, they were simply "Daddy Fred's and Momma Belle's" family.

THE FAMILY OF JACK & ERMA

Jack (Edmund Leland) Glascock married Erma Stella Taylor on November 30, 1933. They had intended to be married on the evening of November 29th, by Lloyd Sapp. However, Lloyd got to talking to somebody and didn't get there until after midnight. So in the early morning hours of November 30th, Jack and Erma were married—technically a day later than they planned.

 Jack and Erma added two granddaughters to Daddy Fred's and Momma Belle's family. Italene was born September 24th of 1934, the first great-grandchild of Grandpa Jimmy and Grandma Maggie. Martha Karen arrived on the 24th of June in 1945. Italene  ended up being called "Ikey" as Martha couldn't pronounce her name as a little child. Jack was not called to service during the Second World War, probably for health reasons. He had contracted typhoid fever as a youth, had poor eyesight, and already had dentures.

His daughter, Martha, remembers the time Jack was bitten by a rattlesnake while helping Daddy Fred around the corn crib. The snake bit him on the hand. His dad cut the "x" where each of the fangs had punctured and sucked what blood and poison out as best he could. They then loaded Jack up in a wagon and rushed to Ashland to the doctor. Later in life, Martha remembers what she called a "crazed look" in her dad's eyes as he killed a snake with his lawn mower.

Despite the challenges of health, Jack and Erma still lived an active life. They were both teachers early in their married life, as Jack did not care for the farm life at all (not surprising considering the incident with the rattlesnake!) They moved to Auxvasse, Missouri, to work in a general store. Jack and Erma then moved to Columbia for the rest of their lives.

Jack got a job at McGlasson's Distributing Co. and worked his way up until he was a partner in the company. Perhaps it was because McGlasson's was a candy distributor, but Jack loved children—his own grandchildren and the kids in the neighborhood as well.

Jack and Erma both loved to travel, though they rarely planned a trip. Rather, they decided to go, grabbed a few clothes, hopped in the car and left. Their daughter Martha recalls that at the height of the gas shortages in the 1970's, they decided to drive out to Colorado. They stayed for one day, and then drove back. It was who they were.

Italene was married to Marion Lucas on May 28th, 1957. They added the first great-grandchild for Daddy Fred and Momma Belle with the birth of their first daughter, Amy Adrian Lucas, on April 30th of 1961. A second daughter was soon to follow with the arrival of Susan Alicia Lucas on October 6th, 1962. Italene and Marion then added a son, Scott Jefferson Lucas, who they welcomed into the family on November 17th, of 1964.

Amy would marry Steve Dennison in 2004.

Susan and Charles T. Warren married and bore Italene and Marion their first two grandchildren. Michael Warren arrived on July 14th, 1987. His younger sister, Alexandra Leigh Warren was born on April 4th, 1989.

Scott married Rosaline Lewis in 2001. They have two daughters. Isabel Taylor Lucas was born in 2003. Darcy Fiona Lucas arrived in 2008.

Martha Karen married Kenneth Gregory Geel on June 10th of 1967, and would bring a son and two daughters into the family. David Jeffrey Geel was born on March 7th, 1970. Brandi Kristine Geel arrived on June 11th of 1973. Leslie Kathleen Geel rounded out their family when she was born on March 5th, 1977.

David married Letitia Irene (Tish) Templin on the last day of 1994. They would have two daughters, Annie Claire Geel, born February 7th, 2000, and Lilia (Lily) Grace Geel, who arrived on the 21st of October in 2002.

Brandi was married on January 27th, 1996, to Stephen Laird Marsh. They began their family with a daughter, Emily Taylor Marsh, born January 13th, 1999. Two sons would follow. Clayton Laird Marsh arrived on July 25th of 2001, and his brother, Jack Canfield Marsh, was born November 26th, 2006.

Leslie would marry James Michael Donovan in 2006, on May the 19th, and the couple would add another granddaughter to Martha and Ken: Kinley Reece Donovan, born March 26th, 2010.

Jack and Erma celebrated 50 years of marriage on November 30th, 1983. They were honored with a reception at the Hilton Inn in Columbia in order to celebrate the occasion.

Jack passed away on February 21st, 1990. Erma lived for many more years, before dying on December 9th, 2011. She was 97 years old at the time of her death. They lay together, side-by-side, at Memorial Park in Columbia. They would have four grand-daughters, two grandsons, seven great-granddaughters, and three great-grandsons.

THE FAMILY OF LORANE & BASEY

Lorane, the oldest daughter of Fred and Belle, was also a teacher. She taught at the school in Wilton until she married Basey Vanlandingham, on the last day of the year 1939. They moved to Columbia and lived near the campus while Basey farmed with his father. They would eventually move to his parent's farm. In the 1950's, farming was difficult, and Basey decided to try his hand at a new occupation—politics. He was elected as State Representative from Boone County in 1956, and was re-elected in 1958. In 1960, Basey ran for the State Senate for the 19th district and would serve Boone County there for eight years before retiring.

Lorane and Basey's family would include two sons and a daughter. Arthur Basey Vanlandingham, II, arrived on February 19th, 1943, followed by a second son, Forrest Barry Vanlandingham, born on November 13th, 1945. Their daughter, Becky, came along a few years later in 1953, born on the 1st of August.

A.B., II married Geraldine (Jeri) Crum in 1961, and had two sons. Jeffery Doss Vanlandingham was born on March 2nd, 1962, and followed by Arthur Basey Vanlandingham, III, (known a Jay) who arrived on January 31st, 1964. A.B., II and Jeri were divorced, and A.B. married Zella on February 14th, 1971. A.B. and Zella had two children. Their son, Aric Bryan, was born December 11th, 1972. A daughter, Lisa Lorane, arrived on March 4th, 1978. A.B. would wed a third time, to Bonnie Gail Renfro on May 27th, 2004.

Jay would add a son to the family, when Forrest Avery Vanlandingham was born on August 16th, 1984. Aric would have a son and a daughter. His daughter, Cheyenne Faith Vanlandingham, arrived on September 29th, 1997. His son, Isaak Logan Vanlandingham, was born on May 2nd, 2002.

Lisa Lorane married Robert Gordon Wilkinson, II on July 7th of 2004. They brought two sons into the family. Robert Gordon Wilkinson, III (known as Trey) was born on the 20th of July in 2007. John Silfer Wilkinson, II arrived on February 12th, 2009.

Barry was married three times, first to Sandra Jean Newton, and then to Sharon Fortney. On March 2nd, 2009 he married Nenevie Flores Araojo. Previously Barry and Nenevie had a son, Forrest Wade Vanlandingham, born on the 30th of October in 2006.

Becky Lynn married Robert F. Hall, Jr. on December 20th, 1976. They had two daughters. S. Gabrianna Hall arrived on October 20th, 1981. Her sister, Sallee Gaelle Hall, was born on April 9th of 1985.

Gabrianna and Christopher Neuer were married on July 30th, 2010. Salle married Andrew Jack on June 20th, 2009, and have one son, Jonah Joseph Jack, born on May 14th, 2010.

Basey died on October 26th, 1990. Lorane lived another decade, passing away due to cancer on August 8th, 2000. They are buried together in Columbia Cemetery. Basey and Lorane would leave four grandsons and three granddaughters. Currently they have five great-grandsons and one great-granddaughter.

THE FAMILY OF PUD & BERNIECE

Estil, or "Pud" as he was called, farmed and worked in agriculture his entire life. He married Berniece Begemann in 1941 and the couple had one son, Jerome, who was born in 1944. Pud farmed in Southern Boone County until the 1960's. With times becoming difficult for small family farms, he went to work at the MFA Feed, staying connected to his agricultural roots. They lived on the farm their entire lives.

Jerome grew up in the Ashland area and married Janet Sue Forsee on July 27th, 1963. Jerome became a barber and worked at the Campus Barber Shop in Columbia, until his Uncle Bobbie became ill. Jerome came to work at Bobbie's barber shop in Ashland. After Bobbie's passed away, Bettie gave the barber shop to Jerome. Jerome and Janet had three children—a son and two daughters. Mikel Jerome Glascock was born on October 8, 1966. Betsy Janece Glascock arrived in 1972, on the 15th of August. Leea Jerae Glascock was born on October 26th, 1975.

Mikel, Betsy and Leea were all members of the Missouri High School Rodeo Association. Mike rode as a team-roper. Betsy and Leea both ran barrels and poles. Leea also was breakaway calf-roper. Mike qualified for the National High School Rodeo Team and participated in the National Finals in 1983. Leea also qualified and participated in the National Finals for two consecutive years, in 1993 and 1994. All through these years, Pud and Berniece became Rodeo Grandpa and Rodeo Grandma.

Mikel married Callie Kathryn Langkop. The couple had one daughter, the first grandchild for Jerome and Janet. Ashton Elizabeth was born on February 27th, 1996.

Betsey married Travis Lee Davidson on January 30th, 1999. The family also gained a son on that day—Austin Lee Davison, Travis's son. Betsey and Travis would have a son and a daughter as well. Logan Ray Davidson was born on March 9th, 2000, while Samantha Leann Davidson arrived on December 21st of 2001.

Leea and Jeffrey William Estes were married on October 5th, 2002. They have one daughter, Cray Whitley Estes, who arrived into the family on January 24th, 2007.

Pud died on April 4th, 1993 as the result of an accident on the farm. Berniece would pass away just a few years later, in 1999, on September 25th of that year, from pancreatic cancer. Berniece would live to see her first great-grandchild. Today they lay side-by-side at Woodcrest Cemetery in Ashland. They have left a total of three great-grandsons and two great-granddaughters.

THE FAMILY OF JUDY & WARREN

Judy was the fourth child and second daughter of Fred and Belle. She married Warren Woodson on July 9th, 1939 and moved to Columbia. Warren was a mechanic and they owned a gas station on Route B in Columbia. Judy and Warren had four daughters and one son.

A daughter, Jonna Belle, was born on April 24th, 1940, with their only son, James Warren ("Jimmy") arriving on March 14th of 1942. Mari Ann was born on the 9th of January in 1948. They added two more daughters in the mid-1950's. Connie Jane and Sarah Jean arrived on May 2nd, 1955 and May 10th, 1957 respectively.

Jonna Belle married Robert Franklin Barr on July 31st of 1981.

Jimmy married Martha Chandler in January of 1965 and had two daughters. Lesley Anne Woodson arrived on August 17th, 1965. Kimberly Lynn Woodson was born on July 31st, 1969. After a divorce, Jimmy married Helen Brazzeze in 1977.

Both daughters married and had families of three children. Lesley Anne married Thomas Gregory Steinweg and gave Jimmy three granddaughters. The oldest, Hannah Jane Steinweg, was born March 24th, 1994. A little over a year later, Emery Anne Steinweg was born, on September 8th, 1995. And Claire Elizabeth Steinweg rounded out the family when she arrived on October 29th, 1999.

Kimberly married Jeffrey Dan Mulkey on June 5th, 1993. Their family increased with the birth of a son, Ryan Chandler Mulkey on December 13th, 1995. Their only daughter, Abigail Grace Mulkey, arrived on April 27th, 1998. A second son, Nathaniel George Mulkey, was born on June 19th, 2001.

Mari Ann Woodson married Robert Edwin Bihr on August 16th, 1969. Their family would add two daughters. Rebecca Susan Bihr arrived on November 18th, 1972. Katherine Ann Bihr was born on February 28th, 1979. Mari Ann and Robert were divorced in 1992. Mari Ann married again in 2003, when she wed John William Horstman.

Rebecca married Paul William Brown on the 8th of April, 2006. Katherine wed George B. Robb on July 12th, 2003. Katherine and George have one daughter, Kailey Reese Robb, who arrived on June 27th, 2010.

Connie Jane married Daniel Lee Corman on December 18, 1976. They would have two daughters. Sara Jean Corman arrived on May 2nd, in 1980. Danielle Elizabeth Corman was born on September 9th, 1983. Danielle wed Josh Boehm on July 1, 2008. Two years later Connie and Daniel's first grandchild arrived when Mallory Ann Boehm was born on July 8th, 2010.

Sara Jean married Robert Anthony Simon on March 27th of 1982. They also had two daughters. Emily Jean Simon was born on April 12th, 1985, while Erin Patricia Simon arrived on January 22nd, 1987. Emily married Christopher Brown on December 29th in 2007 and would have two children. A daughter, Isabella Marie Brown, was born on October 19th, 2008. Their son, Joseph Stanislaus Brown, came into the world in 2010, on August 5th.

Warren passed away on September 1st, 1984, at 70 years old. Judy followed him in death from cancer (like so many in the family) nearly a decade later, on July 30th, 1993. Both Warren and Judy were cremated, and their ashes reside today in Memorial Park in Columbia. They would have eight grandchildren—all girls. Those granddaughters would, in turn, produce 3 great-grandsons and 7 great-granddaughters to Judy and Warren.

THE FAMILY OF JUNO & ELLA MAE

Fred Ewell, or "Juno" as he was always called, was the first in the family to make military service his chosen profession. Thus he saw much of the country and the world, including a tour in Korea and two tours in Vietnam during the war. Juno married Ella Mae Pace on March 25th, 1951. Their union produced two daughters for the family.

Theresa Denise Glascock was born on April 13th, 1953, with sister Joella Faye Glascock arriving on the 17th of July in 1954. Juno and Elle Mae were rarely home while he was in the service.

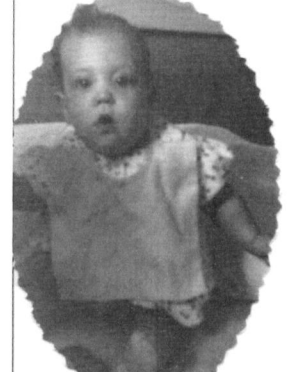

With their dad in the army, Theresa and Joella seemed to be in a different school every year. Both, however graduated from Waynesville High School, near Fort Leonard Wood, this dad's last duty station.

Theresa went to Southwest Missouri State University (now Missouri State) and earned a degree in education. She met her husband, Doug McCouch, there, and they were married on May 25th, 1974. Both became teachers and taught in the Waynesville School District. Theresa taught kindergarten for 24 years and then spent another six years teaching preschool. Doug taught industrial arts in the middle school for nearly two decades, before moving up to be an assistant principal at Waynesville High School. Both are now retired from the teaching profession.

Theresa and Doug's daughter, Christy Allison McCouch, was born April 14th of 1981. In college she studied and earned her degree in entertainment management. She lives in Miami, Florida, now, and is the company manager and assistant to the artistic director at the Actor's Playhouse Theater.

Their son, Benjamin Douglas McCouch, was born on April 12th, 1986. He graduated college with a degree in aerospace engineering and currently works for Hawker/Beechcraft airlines in Wichita, Kansas. Benjamin married Katherine Marie (Katie) Waller on June 5th, 2010.

Joella married Louis Bullington in 1975. After a divorce she was remarried to Charles Sheeley on December 22nd, 1995. She has a step-daughter, Cody Rae Sheeley, who also made Joella and Charles grandparents with his son, Jace Sheeley. Joella passed away on February 25th, 2006, after a battle with lung cancer.

Juno died from lung cancer on October 5th, 1979. He was laid to rest in the Memorial Park Cemetery in Columbia.

THE FAMILY OF MURRY & NANCY

Murry Elston was the sixth child and fourth son of Fred and Belle. Murry left high school to join the U.S. Navy towards the end of the Second World War.

He returned home in 1947 and married Nancy Woolery in 1947, who he knew from school. Murry and Nancy began their family quickly after marriage.

Ronald Murry was born on March 27th, 1948, with Fred William coming along on November 25th, 1949. Murry and Nancy moved back to Columbia briefly (though he continued farming) and while living there, their only daughter, Nancy Louise, arrived on the 15th of December, 1951. The family moved back to the

Anderson place in the bottoms near Wilton. Nancy contracted bronchial pneumonia there and nearly died.

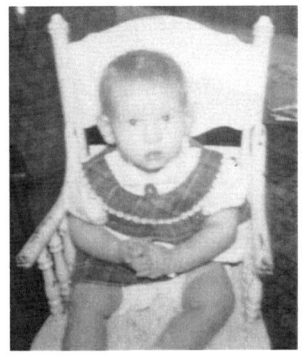

The rest of their family didn't come along for another 12 years. They added two more sons: James Edmund ("Jamie"), who was named after Grandpa Jimmy, was born on June 22nd, 1963, and Herbert Scott (called Scott), arrived on February 2nd in 1965.

Murry farmed for many years while Nancy worked for the State of Missouri down in Jefferson City. They farmed and lived in the Easley Bottoms until about 1950. After returning from a briefly living in Columbia, they moved into a large white two story house in the middle of the bottoms between Wilton and Easley. Nancy recalls the fun she and her brothers had climbing out of the second story windows and jumping off the porch with umbrellas. The old barn was also a source of entertainment and they often rode the cows for fun.

One of the big floods in the 1950's caused them to move out of the bottoms and up on the hill overlooking Goshen and the river. Murry continued to farm but also began working for the state Department of Agriculture. In 1967 he followed his father into politics, and was elected as County Clerk for Boone County. He remained in the position until 1979. Murry and Nancy retired to Arkansas, though he still worked for a friend of his at the Sentinel Wood Treatment Company.

During the years that Daddy Fred and then Murry were in politics, life for the older kids often meant a lot of campaigning during election years. There would be stump speaking events all over the small towns in Boone County. The kids passed out fliers and participated in all the campaigning activities. It also, of course, meant a lot ice cream socials and barbeque stands during the summer campaigns.

Ronald graduated from Ashland High School and married Toni Pollard from Marshall, Missouri. They wed in May of 1968, and lived in Marshall, Missouri. Ronald worked for a trucking company while Toni was a hair dresser. They had a daughter, Carla Renee Glascock, born on May 8th of 1969. Carla would be Murry and Nancy's first grandchild.

A second daughter arrived on January 29th, 1972, with the birth of Teresa Denise Glascock.

Carla would bring two granddaughters for Ronald and Toni. Nicole Lea Blankenship was born on December 4th, 1984. Samantha Danielle Luckett arrived on April 2nd, 1991. Carla is married to Joe Harris. Nicole married Cole Joseph (known as CJ) McQuire and had a son, Cole Joseph McQuire, born December 27th, 2003.

Theresa would bring a grandson and a granddaughter to Ronald and Toni. Kevin Powell arrived into the family on January 30th, 1991. Paris Belle Bigby was born on Independence Day, the 4th of July, in 2004. Teresa was married to Rowdy Bigby, who passed away in 2011.

Fred William also graduated from Ashland High School, and studied for a year at Missouri Valley College. He then went to work for a car dealership in Columbia. He and Vicki Lee Nichols were married in December of 1969. The next year they had their only child, Leigh Ann Glascock, born May 4, 1970.

Fred and Vicki divorced in 1972. Fred then added a son with the birth of Sammy W. Glascock on June 19th, 1978. Today Fred is married to Linda Gail Moody. They wed on June 3rd, in 1995.

Leigh Ann married Brian Thomas on October 16th, 1993 and they had a son, Spencer Dale Thomas, born on September 19th, 1997. Leigh Ann and Brian were divorced several years later.

Nancy Louise, like her brothers, graduated from Ashland and then went to work for a lawyer in Columbia. On March 7th, 1970 she married Derwood Tracy. She then went to work for the State of Missouri in Jefferson City, beginning a career even though she didn't know that at the time. She moved into several different positions within the state (a common occurrence for state workers!), before ending up at the Mid-Mo Mental

Health Center as the secretary to the Assistant Superintendent of Administration. She stayed there for 21 years in various roles, ending up as a Department Head of purchasing, communications, transportation and laundry.

Nancy and Derwood had their first child in 1970 when Kelly Irene Tracy was born on the 28th of September. A second daughter, Angela Marie Tracy, was born on September 8th, 1976. Their final child, another daughter, was born on December 20th, 1982. Kalynn Tracy has the distinction of no middle name as her parents never came up with a suitable middle name that liked to go with Kalynn.

Nancy continued working in different capacities for the state of Missouri. She moved to the Department of Corrections and ended as the Business Manager at the Algoa Correctional Center in Jefferson City. Amidst all of this, Nancy was divorced in 1990. She married Robert Bryant then on September 12th of 1992. Nancy retired from the state in 2001. In 2004, she and Robert packed up everything and moved to Warsaw, Missouri, on a quiet end of the Lake of the Ozarks in order to truly enjoy retirement.

Kelly was an athletic child and played both softball and basketball at Ashland. In her junior season, she was part of the girl's state championship softball team. She went to college at Lincoln University, where she would earn degrees in Coaching and Education. She would eventually earn a Master's degree in Education.

Kelly married Will Randle in October of 1992. Their first child, a daughter, Kelsey Elaine, was born on October 31st, 1995—a Halloween baby. Their son, Jamison Day Randle, arrived on June 29, 1998. They added another daughter, Emma Grey Randle on April 30th, 2008. Little Emma is said to be the image of her great-grandmother, Nancy. Kelly teaches in the New Bloomfield School District. Will is a forensic chemist for the Missouri State Highway Patrol, and teaches a class in forensic science at Columbia College.

Angela was a much different child than her older sister. She was not interested in sports nearly so much as Kelly. She went into nursing. After graduating from Southern Boone County High School, she worked part-time for Boone County Hospital, went to Columbia College and earned a degree in Marketing. She is currently in Nursing School and is scheduled to graduate in May of 2013 as a Registered Nurse.

Angela married Martin Shultz on October 18th, 1997. Their first child, Alexander Martin Shultz, was born on February 7th of 2001. They added a daughter, Addie Elizabeth Shultz on July 5th, 2005.

Kalynn also grew up in Ashland and graduated from Southern Boone County High School. She went to college in Springfield for a year, and then transferred to the University of Missouri in Columbia. She earned a degree first in General Studies before returning to school to add a bachelor's degree in Nutrition. Kalynn was married to Josh Ramsey on March 8th, 2008. Kalynn and Josh added two great-grandsons to Murry and Nancy. Samuel Weston Ramsey was born on February 2nd, 2010. Benjamin Cash Ramsey arrived September 7th, 2011.

When Murry and Nancy moved to Arkansas, the younger brothers, Jamie and Scott, moved with them. They both would graduate from Herber Spring High School.

Jamie went to work at the Sentinel Wood Treatment. He is a semi-truck driver now. Jamie married Donna Beth Pollard on June 14th, 1985. Donna is a Forest Ranger in Herber Springs, where she manages the visitor center at the John F. Kennedy Lookout Center. In 1990 Jamie and Donna became the proud parents of their only child, Katharyn Leigh Glascock. Katy, as she is usually called, arrived July 2nd, 1990.

Scott went to Batesville College after high school, where he earned his degree. He went to work for Wal-Mart as the Assistant Director of warehouse facility in Searcy, Arkansas. He married Angie Goble on August 15th, 1987. Scott and Angie's first child would be the only grandson for Murry and Nancy. Matthew Scott Glascock was born on May 4th, 1992, just a short time before Murry would pass away. But Murry did live to see and hold his only grandson.

Scott and Angie added a daughter to the family when Saralyn Megan Glascock was born on July 8th of 1994. Scott moved to Michigan to work for Wal-Mart distribution shortly after he and Angie were divorced. Scott remarried on October 1st, 2010, when he wed Yanina (Yo) Rios.

Murry and Nancy would leave a family of 8 granddaughters, 1 grandson, 6 great-grandsons and 6 great-granddaughters, with more to surely join their family in the coming years.

Murry and Nancy enjoyed their quiet life in Arkansas. They reached 45 years of marriage. Murry contracted cancer and died on July 12th, 1992. Nancy would live on until Easter Sunday, April 4, 1999 when she passed away due to aneurism. They are buried together under a shade tree in the Chastain Chapel Cemetery in Tumbling Shoals, Arkansas.

THE FAMILY OF BOBBIE & BETTIE SUE

Bobbie was the seventh and last child of Fred and Belle. Nicknamed, "Rube," he married Bettie Sue Garrett on May 24th, 1949.

Initially they farmed, but in 1957 Bobbie decided to embark on a different career and went to the Mohler Barber School in Kansas City. They moved back to Columbia, and he went to work at the Campus Barber Shop. They moved back to Ashland in 1960 and he opened his own barber shop.

Bobbie and Bettie Sue had two sons and a daughter. Bobbie Elmore, Jr. was born on April 3rd, 1950. Their daughter, Pamela Lee Glascock, arrived on June 30th of 1953. John Duane Glascock was born then on May 6th, 1959.

Bobbie, Jr. married Cynthia Louise Hackman on July 6th, 1969. Their family would include two girls and a boy. The oldest, Susan Elizabeth arrived on September 23rd,

1973. Their son, Chad Elliott, was born July 27th, 1975. And their family was rounded out when Erin Lynn was born on the 29th of January in 1979.

Susan would marry Brian Keith Tutt on February 12th, 1994. They would add a son and a daughter to the family. Lydia Jade Tutt was born on November 24th, 2000. Adam Jeffrey Tutt came along on the 7th of September in 2002.

Chad married Wendy Gale Singer on the 3rd day of May, 2003. They also would have a son and a daughter. Grayson Thomas Glascock was born on August 23rd, 2006, while little sister Laken Emery Glascock arrived on November 2nd, 2008.

Erin married John Landon Hargis in 2002, on the 2nd of April. They would give Bobbie and Cindy three more grandchildren. Trenton Elliott Hargis arrived in September, on the 2nd, of 2004. Blaine Elmore Hargis made it two boys for Erin and John, when he was born on January 2nd, 2006. Their daughter, Courtney Jo Hargis, was then born on October 2nd, 2008.

Pam added three more granddaughters to Bobbie and Bettie's family. Her first, Nicole Lee Glascock was born on June 6th, 1972. After a marriage to William Lasniewski, Pam married Ricky Howe on June 13th, 1977. They would have two daughters. The oldest, Emmy Lou Howe, arrived on November 19th, 1977. Her younger sister, Sarah Elizabeth Howe, was born on the 16th of July in 1982. Pam and Ricky were divorced in 1990. Pam is now married to William Slama. They were wed on December 29, 1998.

Nicole married David Fleetwood Anderson on May 22nd, 2004. The next year, on October 4th, Nicole and David had their first son, Henry Thomas Anderson. A second son, Cooper William Anderson, arrived on December 30th, 2006. They added another grandson for Pam, when Dillon Fleetwood Anderson was born on the 1st of November in 2011. David is currently in the U.S. Army, and is stationed at Fort Sam Houston in Texas.

Pam's granddaughter came from the marriage of Emmy to Aaron Andrew Guinn on June 26th, 1998. Their daughter, Whitney Nicole Guinn, was welcomed into the family on January 14th, 1999.

Sarah married Jacob Martin Myers on June 7th, 2008. Jacob is in the U.S. Army and is currently serving in Afghanistan. This is his third tour overseas, following two tours in Iraq. Sarah lives in Colorado Springs, Colorado, near Fort Carson, where Jacob is stationed when stateside.

John married Sara Beth Inglish on May 17th, 1980. They would have a son and a daughter to add to the family. John Duane Glascock II was born on March 20th, 1984. Their daughter, Jaclyn Shea Glascock, arrived on May 24th, 1988. John and Sara divorced in 1989. John then married Sandy Randall in 1992; they were divorced in 1999. On November 21st, 1999, John married Kristen Erin Gerber. John and Kristen have a daughter, Katelin Erin Glascock, born January 21st, 2001.

Bobbie and Bettie Sue lived on the farm on Liberty Lane until Bobbie passed away on May 15th, 1973. He died of cancer at only 45 years of age. He was buried at Woodcrest Primitive Baptist Church in Ashland.

Bettie would survive Bobbie by over 30 years, passing away on the last day of May in 2006. Like her husband, she too succumbed to cancer. She was laid to rest beside Bobbie at Woodcrest. Bobbie and Bettie left a family of 2 grandsons and 8 granddaughters, plus 7 great-grandsons and 4 great-granddaughters.

The family of "Daddy Fred" and "Momma Belle" now number a total 190 persons. 129 of these are direct descendants of Grandpa Jimmy and Grandma Maggie. Fred and Belle would have 7 children, 21 grandchildren, 45 great-grandchildren, 54 great-great-grandchildren, and 1 great-great-great-grandchild.

MAY 1960

CHAPTER EIGHT:

The Family of John & Stella Glascock

John Sterling Glascock arrived to the family of James and Margaret on September 24, 1889, just two days shy of the second birthday of his older brother. It was the closeness of the birthdays of these two young babies that would eventually decide the timing of our family reunion. Both Fred and John would more closely resemble their Dad, who was slight of build.

Four states--Washington, Montana, North and South Dakota—entered the union in 1889. The first tabulating machine was patented in January. Benjamin Harrison was inaugurated as the 23rd president. The Eiffel Tower opened in Paris, to commemorate the French Revolution. As with any year in those early days of Grandpa Jimmy's and Grandma Maggie's family, news of events and advancements such as these might have been interesting, but bore little practical use for the time being.

John grew up on the family farm and grew to become a farmer himself. His world in those childhood years consisted of the farm. Travel meant going to his grandpa's farm or any of the homes of nearby family. He, as his brothers and sisters, spent time visiting and staying with family throughout Ashland and Wilton.

John fell in love with a young woman who lived close, Stella Elizabeth Crump. She was one of four sisters, and just a couple of years younger than John.

They were married on November 20, 1910. Three years later John and Stella were looking forward to the birth of their first child. The young baby girl though was stillborn on August 5, 1913. For the young parents and the family this was heartbreaking. Despite the loss, John and Stella still hosted that year's birthday dinner.

By the next year, Stella was pregnant again. Dorothy Frances Glascock was born to them on September 22nd of 1914. This bouncing baby girl was the second granddaughter added to the family that year.

John farmed most of his life. Stella kept house and, assuredly, helped on the farm as well. Alberta, one of their grandchildren remembers visiting the farm. Almost always

there seemed to be an "egg pie" (custard) waiting with perhaps some leftover fried chicken. She'd wake up on a winter morning and snuggle down under several quilts, while she listened as her "Papa John" put wood in the stove to start warming the house. Breakfast was often fried chicken with biscuits and gravy. She might spend the day shucking corn or help her grandma—who she called "Mom"— churning and making butter. The old smokehouse always smelled like curing meat, particularly if they had just butchered a hog. Wednesdays meant a trip to Columbia to the John King Market. A loaf of bread and a loaf of bologna to go along with it meant sandwiches to eat on the way home.

Dorothy grew into a young woman and married Wayne Gilpin on the 25th of April in 1936. Unfortunately they would share a common experience with John and Stella—their first child, a son, died at birth. But two daughters would be born into their family.

Alberta Jane Gilpin arrived on March 11th of 1942. Three years later, on the 22nd of November of 1945, Marthetta

Lane arrived. Alberta and Marthetta grew up in the loving homes of their parents and grandparents.

Tragedy continued in John and Stella's family however. Marthetta, as a young girl of ten or eleven, was diagnosed with a malignant brain tumor in 1956. The family briefly moved to Kansas City for surgery and treatment. At the time, those types of treatments simply were not available in Central Missouri. After three months in Kansas City, they returned to Columba and Marthetta went into Boone Hospital. Marthetta would finally succumb to her cancer in March of 1957.

After Marthetta's death, Dorothy and Wayne purchased an old house and began to remodel it. They "gutted" the house and worked tirelessly to refinish it. It seemed to Alberta to be as much therapeutic as anything.

John and Stella celebrated their fiftieth wedding anniversary in November of 1960. Dorothy and Wayne hosted it in their home. The family gathered to congratulate the couple. Dorothy, who worked sometimes as a cake decorator, made the cake. Several of John and Stella's nieces served at the reception.

Two years later, in 1962, Stella had to have her leg amputated and at that time John retired from farming. They left the farm and built a new house on a large lot where Dorothy and Wayne lived. Stella Elizabeth Glascock passed away on June 23rd of 1962. She was buried at the cemetery at New Liberty Primitive Baptist Church. John lived another five years. In July of 1967 he became ill and was admitted into Boone Hospital. He died a week later, on the 19th of the month. He would be buried besides Stella in New Liberty.

Life continued for Dorothy and Wayne. Both worked at a series of jobs through their lives. For a while Dorothy owned Ashland Café. She also spent time as a daycare provider and dabbled in politics as a committeewoman. Wayne was a farmhand early in life, and later operated a filling station and drove a truck for Phillips 66 gasoline. Wayne was also active in the Ashland Masonic Lodge and both of them were members of the Order of Eastern Star in Ashland.

Dorothy and Wayne celebrated 35 years of marriage in 1971. Unfortunately, in the next year, Dorothy suffered a series of strokes, before passing away on New Year's Day in 1973. A year later, Wayne re-married a life-long friend, Mary Coonce Burnett. Wayne lived for many years after that, though in the 1990's his health began to decline. He died on July 8th, 1996.

During these years Alberta would attend the University of Missouri, graduating in 1965. She then attended the New Orleans Baptist Theological Seminary and graduated in 1967. Alberta went to work for the Missouri Baptist Convention, working over 33 years. She retired in 2002. She did not, however, retire from life or additional work! Alberta taught 7th-grade writing at the Southern Boone County high school for a year, and then became the Director of Education and Ministry at the Parkade Baptist Church in Columbia.

Alberta never married, but she did have a family. She built a new house in Jefferson City in 1985, and felt it was large enough for her to share it. She began the process of sponsoring a refugee family. In April of 1986, Tudor and Maria Rafa, escaped refugees from the Communist Regime in Romania came to live with her. Tudor and Maria had swam the Danube River to escape, and were forced to leave their two children behind. Alberta helped them to get their children out legally. It took nearly a year-and-a-half, but on July 5th of 1987, Alberta and her new family met the children in New York City. They lived with her for five years before striking out on their own.

One of the children, Calin, would marry another Romanian, Flori, and add a young daughter, Kaylee, to their family. Just this past July, a son, Zayden, arrived. Alberta now lives with them, in Ashland, in a basement apartment that affords her plenty of opportunities to baby-sit. Tudor and Maria live just a few minutes away. Their other child, Ramona, married Dustin Schatzer, and they have two children, Alexa and Isaac. They also live in the country just outside Ashland.

In Alberta's own words:

> "And, so with me the John Sterling Glascock "line" with end. But what wonderful family memories I have been blessed with. God has been faithful and good just as He promised."

While Alberta is correct that the blood line will end, it does seem that the spirit of her family and our family will continue through the lives of another family who risked everything to come to America and ended up among us.

CHAPTER NINE:

The Family of Ross & Lola Glascock

Ross Nowlin was born into the Glascock family on February 4, 1894. James & Margeret lived on their farm just to the south and west of Ashland, often call the Oldham area. The world into which he was born would have seemed to us as rather slow-moving and sedate. Yet plenty happened in the world that first year of life that would change the life of young baby Ross. Later that month, war broke out in Cuba as the Cubans rebelled against Spanish rule, a conflict into which America would eventually be drawn. Inventions that year included "liquid air" and "x-rays." And while it is doubtful young Ross even noticed it, a 6.6 earthquake hit Missouri, centered on the New Madrid fault near Charleston, Missouri.

Ross's middle name, Nowlin, came from the maiden name of his great-grandmother, Margaret Nowlin Devin. Margaret married Shadrick Mustain. Their daughter, Lucy, would marry Franklin Ewing Glascock. They were the parents of James Edmund Glascock, Ross's father.

No one remains who can tell us what his childhood was like, but we know he was raised on the family farm and we know enough of what life on a farm in the early twentieth century to have a good idea of how those early years went. The work was hard, and assuredly young Ross helped out just as soon as he was old enough. As he grew he would have had different chores in the fields and with the livestock. Farming in the rural Missouri in the early twentieth century was a difficult profession that simply did not afford much in the way of money and wealth. In bad years, life could come down to hand-to-mouth.

His formal education went up through the eighth grade. He surely travelled as far as Columbia and Jefferson City, but it would be doubtful he ever went much further in those years. This was before automobiles and a trip even to just St. Louis or Kansas City would have entailed several days of travel. So Ross grew up close to home, and the world remained a mystery to him. At least, that is, until he entered the military in 1917.

Ross found himself in the U.S. Army in 1917, stationed in Waco, Texas. World War I was coming to a climax and America was continuing to send young men "over there." But Ross was never sent overseas, instead staying in Waco for those many months. The war ended in November of 1918.

He stayed in Waco until sometime in 1919 before returning home to the farm to marry Lola Catherine Sapp on the last day of November in 1919. Ross and his brother Fred had bought a farm near Wilton, and Ross and Lola set up their home in what was called the "little house" on that farm.

Before their first anniversary Ross and Lola had a baby—Reba Ethlyn, born on October 8, 1920. Early in her life it was evident that Reba (or "Pid" as she was called) had serious health problems. She was what was called a "blue baby"—the diagnosis from the doctors was that she had a hole in her heart. Today, surgery could correct that problem, but that was simply not an option in the 1920's. Nonetheless she lived into her late teenage years.

Their only son was born early in 1922. Douglas Oswald Glascock, or "Buddy" as everyone called him, came into the world on February 26, 1922. Another daughter, Helen Louise, was born on November 23, 1923. Not quite four years after that a third daughter was born into the home of

 Ross and Lola, Ola Mae, on May 13, 1927. And a fifth child came five years later when Betty Jane was born on May 16, 1932.

Raising a family on a farm in the 1920's was challenging to say the least. Farm prices were depressed long before the "Great Depression" made it official for everyone else. The work was still back-breaking as virtually all work was still done by hand and by animal power, and the rewards sometimes meager. The onset of the Great Depression certainly did not help the financial situation.

 During the depression, the family moved off the farm and into a house right in Wilton. It was there, in June of 1939, that the heart defect in "Pid" claimed her life. She was eighteen years old at the time of her death.

Ross & Lola moved back to the family farm in 1941 when Grandma Maggie died. Jimmy and Maggie had moved out to the farm when it was originally bought. Ross and his dad continued to work the farm while Ross and Lola raised their family. But the financial struggles finally convinced them to make a dramatic change in occupation. Ross was appointed as the postmaster of Hartsburg, Missouri. The change was not without controversy as Grandpa Jimmy was dead set against it and wanted Ross to continue working the farm with him. But Ross had made up his mind that he needed to do this for his family. Finally, Ross reached his limit with his father, and told him, in no uncertain terms, that he was taking the job and moving his family to Hartsburg. If his dad wanted to come with them fine. If not though, Grandpa Jimmy needed to figure out who else he was going to live with! The discussion was thus over and Ross, Lola, and the girls, moved to a house in Hartsburg.

Originally the post office in Hartsburg was located is what is now the American Legion Hall. Ross bought what was known as the "bank building" there at the main intersection in Hartsburg and convinced the postal service to move the post office into the bottom floor. The post office occupied the ground floor and the family lived upstairs.

By then, the children were beginning to leave the nest and start their own families. Already Buddy had married Rosa "Bodie" Hickam on New Year's Day in 1942. Helen married Joseph Smith on November 23rd of 1945 and her younger sister, Ola Mae, then married Robert Taggart a few weeks later, on January the 12th of 1946, while Robert was on  leave from the Navy. They married on the 12th, and he then had to leave on the 13th to return to duty. He came home for good that following May.

Only Betty Jane remained at home as they settled into life in above the new post office. With Buddy, Helen and Ola Mae married, grandchildren were soon to follow. And the next few years saw several arrive!

Barrett Lee Glascock was born on December 3, 1946 to Buddy and Bodie, becoming the first grandchild of Ross and Lola. Lonnie Ross Taggart, the firstborn son of Robert & Ola Mae, followed, came into the world on April 24, 1947. The first granddaughter was also born to Buddy and Bodie on January 21, 1948, when Brenda Kay Glascock arrived. Buddy and Bodie's second son, David Bruce Glascock, was born May 25, 1949. The decade closed out when Robert Michael Taggart (always called "Mike") was born to Robert & Ola Mae on August 11, 1949.

The family kind of caught their breath for a year or so, but more grandkids were coming. Robert and Ola Mae welcomed their third son into the family when Roger Rex Taggart ("Rex" to the family) was born on June 5, 1951. The next year, Beverly Glascock became the second granddaughter, when she was born to Buddy and Bodie on February 13, 1952.

So far, the grandchildren had solely been from Buddy and Bodie, and Robert & Ola Mae. That was about to change. Helen and Joe had their first child, Donna Gail Smith, on October 27, 1954. Bonita Sue Glascock, the fifth child of Buddy and Bodie, arrived on August 24, 1955. Donna and Bonita made four granddaughters for Ross and Lola. And even though there were still several other grandchildren to arrive, Donna and Bonita would be the last of the girls! The family of Ross and Lola was about to have another growth spurt of grandsons.

Betty Jane left home when she married Noel "Ed" Blythe on March 12, 1954. They began their family in 1958, when Noel Edward Blythe, Jr. was born on June 14, 1958—a Flag Day baby. Helen and Joe welcomed their first son into the family on January 21, 1959 when Richard Allan Smith (always called Dick) arrived. Later that summer Betty and Ed had a second son, Kendall Eugene Blythe, born August 26, 1959. Helen and Joe added another son to the family when Douglas Leo Smith was born on July 27, 1960. And finally, Paul Edmund Blythe arrived to Betty and Ed on January 30th of 1962—the last of the grandchildren of Ross and Lola. Through their four children, they had seen their family increase and be blessed with fourteen grandchildren. Four granddaughters and ten grandsons made up a new generation of the Glascock family through Ross and Lola.

Ross remained postmaster in Hartsburg until he retired in 1962. He was named Postmaster of the Year for Missouri that year. During their years in Hartsburg, Ross and Lola would be founding members of the American Legion Post in Hartsburg. And they would live through one of the biggest floods of the Missouri River in 1951. Water reached the backyard of the post office, but didn't get in the building. It would take the great flood of 1993 for that to happen!

Upon retirement, Ross and Lola moved up to Ashland, to a little house on Broadway that still stands. They enjoyed their final years together with family all around. That little white house became the center of Ross and Lola's family. Whether just stopping in to say "hi" or everyone gathering for a family occasion, that house was the point on which the Ross and Lola's family centered.

In 1969, Ross and Lola celebrated their golden wedding anniversary. Ross insisted (in fact was adamant) that the celebration take place on the actual day. So the family gathered on Sunday, November 30, 1969, fifty years to the day, at Goshen Church to celebrate the occasion. Cake and punch were served to the many well-wishers and enjoyed a family dinner after the reception. Buddy, Helen, Ola Mae and Betty Jane presented their mother with a family ring and their father with a tie pin. Each had their birthstones set into the piece. Ross gave Lola three pieces of jewelry, while Lola gave Ross a golden wedding band—his first after fifty years of marriage!

Unfortunately Ross would have little time to wear that ring. In the middle of December of 1969, Ross suffered a debilitating stroke. He would linger for over three months, spending his time in the hospital and then a nursing home. Ross passed away on April 5, 1970. On the morning of his funeral another great-grandchild was born, girl, Lisa, to Lonnie and Judy Taggart. Lisa Rachell Taggart entered the world early that morning to bring a ray of joy to time of sadness. Ross was buried in the cemetery on the hill at Goshen Church in Wilton, where he centered so much of his life.

Grandma Lola had many productive years left, and continued living in the little white house there in Ashland. She watched as her family continued to grow. The grandkids continued to grow up and marry, and she would see more and more great-grandchildren enter her family. Lola stayed in good health right up to the last year or so of her life, and continued living on her own until her death. Lola also suffered a stroke in the spring of 1991. She remained in the hospital for about a month, before joining Ross on May 17th of 1991, at the age of 92. Lola was laid to rest beside Ross at the Goshen Cemetery.

THE FAMILY OF BUDDY & BODIE

Buddy (Douglas Oswald) was the second child and only son of Ross and Lola, coming into the world in February of 1922. Buddy grew into a big, strapping young man, and eventually caught the eye of Rosa Ellen "Bodie" Hickam. They were married on New Year's Day in 1942 (though they really intended to be married on New Year's Eve) and lived in St. Louis where Buddy worked for an ordnance factory until he left for the service in November of 1942. He was in the signal corps and spent time in the states and in England. He came home for good in early 1946.

When Buddy returned, they moved to Columbia and immediately began their family. The oldest son, Barrett, was born in December of 1946, followed by their oldest daughter, Brenda, in January of 1948 and a second son, Bruce, in May of 1949. They waited a couple more years before adding a second daughter, Beverly, in February of 1952 and then a third daughter, Bonita, who was born in August of 1955. Even while living in Columbia, Buddy and Bodie were very active at Goshen Church, making the trip from Columbia each Sunday. Their children remain just as active today.

1956

While living in Columbia, Buddy and Bodie ran a grocery store at the corner of Broadway and Third Street (now Providence Road) for many years. As the family grew, they eventually moved to Ashland, where both Buddy and Bodie were active in the community. Buddy helped in the early days of the Ashland Optimist Club in the 1960's, and stayed active in it his entire life. He served a term as Governor of the Missouri District in 1979-80. In 1988 Buddy was the first recipient of the "Citizen of the Year" at the Ashland Fall Festival. Buddy was ill at the time and was unable to accept in person (he would pass away shortly afterwards.) Today a scholarship in his name is still sponsored by the Optimist Club for local students.

Bodie was no less active. Brenda recalls her mother talking about being the leader of at least four different youth organizations in a single year. Her civic involvement would also lead to her being named "Citizen of the Year" in Ashland as well.

Buddy and Bodie's family grew. While he was the oldest, Barrett would marry last. Barrett married Beth Manning Newell on May 23rd of 1981. When Barrett and Beth married they also added a step-daughter, Erica Elizabeth Manning, to the family. Their family would grow with the arrival of two sons as well. Brandon Lee Glascock was born on January 26th of 1984. Nicholas Barrett Glascock arrived on September 12^{th,} 1985. Barrett owns the Glascock Agency in Ashland, and continues as an insurance agent there. Barrett also joined the Ashland Optimist Club at the same time as his dad, and remains active there still. Barrett would also serve as secretary of the club for over 25 years, plus two terms as President. He also served as the Governor of the East Missouri District for the Optimist Clubs, from 2002-03.

Erica went to the University of Missouri and attained a degree in Parks and Recreation Management. She moved to St. Louis for work, met her future husband there. She married Ben Canlas on June 26th, 2004 and the couple moved back to Columbia. They have a daughter, Ava Elizabeth Canlas, who was born on April 16th, 2006, and a son, Benjamin Tate Canlas, who arrived on May 7th, 2010. Erica is currently a stay-at-home mom, while Ben works for the University of Missouri.

Brandon went to the Ozarks Technical College after high school, and graduated with a degree in Fire Science. He then went to the University of Central Missouri, where he earned a bachelor's degree in business, and is now working on an MBA from Columbia College. Brandon currently works as a loan officer with Boone County Bank, and has begun running marathons.

Nicholas graduated from the University of Missouri with a degree in Nutrition and Fitness. He then went on to the Sinclair School and Nursing and is now a Registered Nurse working in the Intensive Care Unit at the University Hospital in Columbia. He married his high school sweetheart, Jackie, on January 3rd, 2009. Jackie is currently working on her PhD in Genetics Research at Mizzou. Both are avid Tiger fans!

Brenda married Lloyd Wayne Wilson on June 25th, 1966. They would have two daughters, Michelle Kay (Shelley) Wilson, born April 21st, 1969, and Lori Wilson, who arrived on September 7th of 1973. Brenda has been active in the Ashland Rainbow Girls and Eastern Star. For 22 years she served as Mother Advisor in the Rainbow Girls, plus as State Dean of the Grand Cross of Color. She also has served in several state positions in Eastern Star, including Worthy Grand Matron for Missouri in 2008. She also has been the clerk for Goshen Church for many years, a position which her grandfather, Ross, held. Brenda and Wayne divorced in 1983. She remarried on July 2nd, 1994, to Leslie Clay Austin.

Shelly went to Williams Woods College and earned a bachelor's degree in Business. She worked for Landmark Bank for several years, along with selling real estate. She now is a Senior Accountant with the University of Missouri System Accounting Office. She married Myron Dean Helms on April 11th, 1992. Their union has produced three children. Jordan Michelle Helms was born in 1994, on July 20th. A son came next, Tanner Douglas Helms, who arrived on June 2nd, 1997. Another daughter was born in 2003, when Ellie Elizabeth Helms arrived on September 16th. All three children keep their parent busy with church youth group, PTA, and soccer. Shelley also loves scrapbooking.

Lori Sue graduated from Southern Boone County High School and then attended Columbia College. She earned an Associate's Degree there, in General Studies. She worked in Kansas City for the Division of Probation and Parole before returning to Mid-Missouri and working at the University Hospital for several years.

Early in life, Bruce Glascock had a love for horses. Even before the family left Columbia, where there was no place to keep a horse, Bruce had saved enough money to buy his first. Virgil and Virginia Wren let him pasture it on their farm. He was instrumental in bringing PRCA rodeo to Ashland and served as the chairman of the chapter in Ashland. Bruce attended Farrier School in Oklahoma and shoed horses on the side for many years. Bruce also worked at the Pizza House in Columbia as a teenager (along with his brother Barrett and cousin Perry McDonald), and is still known among his family for his homemade pizza. Though now retired, Bruce keeps busy working at the Callaway Sale Barn, where he works with his horse.

Bruce married Donna Kay Benedict on March 25th, 1969. Their son, Kevin Dale Glascock, arrived on September 27th, 1969. Then, in 1973, Bruce and Donna added two new babies to the family, when they were blessed with twin girls—Jennifer Lynn and Jeanette Jo. They were born on February 2nd, 1973. All three of Bruce's children grew up with their dad's passion for rodeo and horses. Bruce would also serve in the Missouri High School Rodeo Association, including several terms as president of the association. He also was Missouri's representative to the national association for several years. Locally he was chairman of the Ashland Rodeo Committee for several years as well.

Upon graduating from high school, Kevin attended a diesel mechanic school in Arizona. He worked for MODOT for many years, and has recently taken a position with a private company in Sedalia, Missouri. He married Kelly White on September 30th, 1995. They have one son, Kohl David Glascock, who arrived on June 27th, 2004. They live in Syracuse, Missouri.

Jennifer attended the University of Missouri and earned a degree in Early Childhood Development. She works in the training department of Shelter Insurance. She married Steve Tade on July 8th, 1995. They also have one son, Riley Steven Tade, born January 24th, 1999.

Jeannette moved to Texas after high school to work on a ranch for a couple of years. She returned to Ashland and married Gerry Lisby on November 30th of 1996. They had a daughter, Taylor Jo Lisby, who arrived on March 28th of 2001. Jeanette and Gerry would divorce in 2009. Jeanette then married to Dustin Jelik, on the 25th of May of 2010. They currently live in Kansas.

Beverly married Jesse Steelman in 1974, and added yet another set of three sons to the family. Shawn Dewayne Steelman was born in 1972. Shannon Dale arrived in 1975. Younger brother Scott Douglas came along in 1980. Bev inherited her mom's talent for cake decorating. Both Bodie and Bev have made all kinds of birthday, anniversary, and wedding cakes for a wide range of people. Bev has also been active in the Eastern Star and enjoys scrapbooking. And despite having only sons, also helped with Rainbow Girls. Everyone in the family are race car enthusiasts.

Shawn married Jamie Metcalf on March 15th, 2008. This union brought three step-children into the family: Maridath, Fletcher, and Johnna. Shawn has worked at Sentinel Lumber and Hardware for many years. Jamie works for the Southern Boone County School District. Maridath is currently attending William Woods College, where she is working to earn her bachelor's degree in Equestrian Administration. Fletcher is a freshman at Southern Boone where he plays football and plays in the band. And Johnna is a seventh-grader where she is active in band and in gymnastics.

Shannon and Faith Sturms were married on November 17th, 2001. They have a son and a daughter. Hayden Ross Steelman arrived on September 16th, 2003. Reese Ellen Steelman followed her brother into the family on July 25th, 2006. Shannon and Faith met while Faith was doing her student teaching in Ashland, where she remained to teach second and third grades. In 2008 Shannon and a partner began the Steel-Net company, which provides the installation of audio/visual equipment, particularly in schools. Hayden is a third-grader this year, while Reese has just begun kindergarten. Shannon also devotes many hours to coaching in Little League, basketball and football.

Scott also brought a daughter into the family, with the birth of Madison Rayne Steelman on October 11th, 2007. Scott lives in New Haven with Madison and her mom, Amber. They both met while working at Wal-Mart in Columbia. Scott seems to have found his calling as a car salesman in Hermann, Missouri, while Amber works at The Children's Factory in Union. They both also work with "Conceal and Carry" classes with the New Haven Police Department.

Bonita, the youngest, married Lenard Dale (Lenny) Lenger on October 25th, 1975. Carrie Beth Lenger, their daughter, was born in 1980, on March 7th. The son, Tyler William Lenger, was born on January 24th, 1983. Bonita, like her sisters, was active in Rainbow Girls. Bonita also worked for several years in the Band Boosters at Southern Boone

County High, including being a chaperone on the band's trip to Florida while Carrie Beth was in the band. Tyler kept her on the go with baseball.

Carrie Beth attended Merrill University in Jefferson City to earn a degree in cosmetology. She married Cory Robert Fischer on October 28th, 2000. The first son, Boston Cory Fischer, arrived on December 6th of 2002. At the age of 2, he became ill, and was eventually diagnosed with Leigh's Disease. He fought valiantly, but succumbed to the disease on the first day of October in 2006.

Cory and Carrie Beth welcomed a second son into the family, when Jackson Tyler Fischer was born on January 10th, 2009.

Tyler went to school at Central Methodist College on a baseball scholarship. He would earn his bachelor's degree in Recreation Administration.

Buddy died on October the 22nd of 1988. Buddy's Aunt Clarice would pass away on the same day, an hour later than Buddy. He was laid to rest in the Goshen Cemetery. Bodie lived for several more years, enjoying life and several great-grandchildren. She would pass away on December 15th, 2003, and would be buried beside Buddy.

Helen was the second daughter born to Ross and Lola, arriving in November of 1923. Helen, it seemed, was the quiet one of Ross and Lola's family, much like her father in that respect. After high school she attended Central Missouri State University in Warrensburg and was a teacher for several years.

She married Joseph Clifford Smith on November 23rd of 1945, after he returned from the war. Helen and Joe began their family when Donna Gail Smith was born on October 27th of 1954. Two sons would follow. Richard Allen (Dick) Smith arrived on the 21st of January of 1959, quickly followed by Douglas (Doug) Leo Smith on July 27th, 1960.

Helen and Joe lived in Ashland for most of their married lives, mostly on a farm east of Ashland. Both Helen and Joe were members of the Ashland Optimist Club. After retirement both were fixtures at the Optimist Club's bingo nights. Helen baked pies for many years to those nights. Besides farming, Joe was a heavy equipment operator for most of his work life.

Donna not only holds a distinction of not having to change her monogram when she married—but she didn't even have to change to change her last name. Donna and Jim V. Smith were married on June 17th, 1972. Donna has worked as a nurse for many years, while Jim was called into the ministry and continues to serve his congregation in Boone County. Donna and Jim's son, Adam Wayne Smith, arrived on the 11th of April in 1976.

Their daughter, April Lynne Smith, was born almost exactly two years later, on April 27th in 1978.

Adam has a degree in business from the University of Phoenix and is currently working on his MBA. His education helped land him a position in inventory control with Becton/Dickinson, a medical supply company. He married Gaby Valesquez, from Venezuela, on September 17th, 2004. Gaby is a graduate of the University of Nebraska in Industrial Engineering and has an MBA from the University of Phoenix as well. Adam and Gaby currently live in Santa Clara, California.

April went to Central Methodist College, where she met her future husband, Brian Ash. They were wed on May 19th, 2001. April and Brain both teach at Jefferson City High School, and both coach as well. Brian coaches baseball, while April has coached girls' basketball.

Jim and Donna's first grandchild then arrived in 2009, when Nolan Ash was born on the 1st day of May. April works in the Jefferson City Public School District, where she teaches biology and anatomy, and also coaches girl's sports.

Dick graduated from Truman State University with a degree in education. His future wife, Veronica White, also attended Truman and has a degree in education. They were married in June 9th of 1979 and would add two daughters to the family. Lindsey was born on the 17th of September in 1983, while younger sister Whitney was born on September 12th, 1985. Both Dick and Veronica worked as teachers in various school districts around Central Missouri. Dick also spent many years as a basketball coach. At their last stop, Dick would retire from teaching and coaching, while Veronica is now an elementary school principle at the Lake of the Ozarks.

Lindsay went to college at the University of Central Missouri, and, like her parents, earned a degree in education. She taught for a couple of years and then married Austin

Campbell on the 10th of June in 2006. They have a son, Jackson Walker Campbell, who arrived on February 27th, 2009. They then welcomed a daughter, Sawyer Campbell, who was born on the 17th of November, 2011.

Whitney graduated from Missouri Western University in St. Joseph where she was Homecoming Queen. She currently lives in Arizona where she manages a spa.

Doug also attended Truman State University. He currently lives in the Ashland area and works in construction.

Joe died on October 19th, 2009. He was laid to rest in Memorial Park Cemetery in Columbia. Helen has since moved off the farm to a quiet house near her sister Ola Mae in Ashland.

THE FAMILY OF OLA MAE & ROBERT

Ola Mae was born in 1927, the third daughter of Ross and Lola. She also married a man in the service, when she wed Robert Taggart, a U.S. Navy sailor, in 1946. They started their family when he returned from the war, adding three sons. Lonnie Ross Taggart was born in 1947, followed by Robert Michael Taggart (always known as "Mike") in 1949 and Roger Rex Taggart (always called "Rex") in 1951.

Lonnie married Judy Nichols on August 13, 1966. They would have three children (a popular number in the Ross and Lola branch of the family!). Lonna Rene` Taggart was born on March 8th, 1967. A second daughter, Lisa Rachelle Taggart, was born on the

morning of her great-grandpa Ross's funeral—on April 7th, 1970. Finally, Lonnie and Judy added a son, Lance Randall Taggart, who was born on June 23rd of 1975.

Lonnie went to Barber School and has continued to cut hair to this day. While he has worked in a few different shops, most years found him at the barber shop on East Dunklin Street in Jefferson City. Similarly, Judy was a hair dresser.

Lonna married Jeffrey Trammell on April 26th of 1997 in Boone County. Both Lonna and Jeff work for Ameren UE. Lonna and Jeff had a girl and a boy. Brooke Nicole Trammell was born on October 27th of 1998. Braden Jeffrey Trammell came along a couple of years later, arriving on November 3rd of 2000. Braden became the second redhead in the Ross line! Both Brooke and Braden are athletic and keep their parents busy with various sports.

Lisa married Steve Frey on June 20th of 1998, and now live in St. Charles, Missouri. Lisa is an elementary teacher. Steve works for the Boeing Corporation. They also added two children to the family—and again, a boy and a girl. Gavin Frey was born in 1999, on August 13th. Gabrienne Joan Frey arrived on July 24th of 2002. Gavin and his dad both like the outdoors, while Gabrienne loves dancing and the theater.

Lance married Kimberly Gill on October 5th, 1996. Lance followed in his father's footsteps and is a barber. Lance now works in the same shop that Bobbie Glascock and Jerome Glascock worked at in Ashland. And, just like his sisters, he and Kimberley added a grandson and a granddaughter for Lonnie and Judy. Spencer Gill Taggart arrived on the 18th of October in 1998, while younger sister Sayde Lorane Taggart was born on her dad's birthday—June 23rd—in 2002.

Mike married Kay Craig on May 23rd of 1970. Mike and Kay lived in St. Louis where Mike worked as a Registered Nurse. Mike always had a great love of music and played the piano and organ. His musical gift was such that he played almost everything by ear. Kay also did office work in St. Louis. Father's Day in 1974 was a special day for the couple as their first son, Craig Dwayne Taggart was born that June 16th. Another son, Curtis Dale (Curt) Taggart came along about five years later, on January 24th of 1979. A third son, Chad Derek Taggart, was stillborn on  November 23rd of 1984 and is buried in the Sacred Heart Cemetery in Florissant, Missouri.

Craig was active in the theater through high school and pursued a Bachelor's degree in Theater at the University of Missouri in Columbia. He currently lives in California and is trying to break into show business.

Curt married Michelle Margrum from St. Louis, on June 13th of 2006, in Jamica. Curt and Michelle live in Wentzville, Missouri. Curt works for the Master Card Company, while Michelle is an elementary school teacher. They are the parents of two daughters. Lilly Rene Taggart arrived on April 3rd of 2007. Lyla Kay Taggart was born on March 19th, 2010.

Rex spent several years in the U.S. Army. He worked at the University of Missouri for many years as a sheet metal fabricator before retiring.

Rex married Lois Ashlock on June 6th, 1969. They had two children before they were

divorced. Julia Catherine Taggart arrived on the 14th of January in 1970. A son, Mitchell Keith Taggart (known as "Keith") arrived on June 22nd, 1974. Rex then married Catherine Marie (Cathy) Flaim on October 12th, 1985 in St. James, Missouri. Rex and Cathy had one son, Jacob Ross Taggart, who was born on the first day of August in 1986.

Julia had two sons, Dakota Ray Taggart, born on January 12th of 1990, and Dylan William Bailey, who arrived on the 3rd of November, 1997. Julia attended ITT Technical Institute in Kansas City, and currently lives and works in the Kansas City area. Dakota graduated from Southern Boone County High School. Dylan currently attends Southern Callaway High School in Mokane.

Keith followed in his father's footsteps and joined the U.S. Army. He would make military service his career. Keith's first born son was Stephen Mitchell Taggart, born on May 14th, 1999. Keith subsequently married Melissa Williamson on the 23rd of February in 2007, in Columbia. Keith and Melissa met while serving in the army. Their first son, Rex William Taggart, was born in Higginsville, Kentucky, on April 30th, 2009. Their second son, Cash Anderson Taggart, was born on July 25th, 2012, making young baby Cash the newest member of the family of Ross and Lola Glascock.

Jacob Ross went to Southern Boone County High School, and then went to the University of Missouri, where he earned his degree in Nutritional Science. He currently works at the university.

Robert passed away in 1979, on the 29th of May. He was laid to rest at Memorial Park Cemetery in Columbia. Ola Mae worked for over 33 years at the University of Missouri before retiring in 1992. She was awarded the Chancellor's Staff Retiree of the Year award in 2001. This award was presented for her volunteer and community service work after retirement. She was honored with a certificate and monetary gift at the retiree luncheon in April of 2001. She has had many productive years, and to this day, remains a catalyst for this celebration of the 100th reunion.

Just as Robert had died at age 54, Mike also passed away at nearly the same age, being 53 at the time of his death. Mike passed away on the 29th of November, in 2002 in St. Louis. He was laid to rest at the Mount Pleasant Cemetery in Hartsburg, Missouri.

THE FAMILY OF BETTY JANE & ED

Betty Jane was the baby of the family, arriving in May of 1932. Lola originally wanted to name her Bonnie Sue, but that was not to the liking of Grandma Maggie, who wanted Betty Jane. Grandma Maggie's wishes won out (as they usually did), and thus Ross and Lola's baby girl became Betty Jane Glascock.

Like her sisters, Betty Jane married a serviceman. Ed Blythe, from Hartsburg, spent two years in the U.S. Army. They were married on March 12th of 1954, at Goshen Church. While many in the family seemed to migrate north towards Columbia, Ed and Betty went south, and moved to Jefferson City. Betty worked for a while as a bookkeeper for Von Hoffman Press in Jeff City before staying home with the kids. Ed became a plumber and then a pipefitter, working for the Harold G. Butzer Company until his retirement in 1990.

It was four years before Ed and Betty started a family, but when they did, they filled it out in a hurry. Noel Edward, Jr. was born in June of 1958. Kendall Eugene followed less than fifteen months later, arriving in late August of 1959. Paul Edmund made it three brothers in January of 1962.

Ed and Betty raised their family in a house off of Frog Hollow Road, to the southwest of Jefferson City. All three boys graduated from Jefferson City High School. They all three also worked for the local McDonald's restaurants in Jeff City through high school, college, and even beyond. All three also went to Lincoln University in Jefferson City.

Noel was the family redhead, which gave rise to many conflicting claims about where it came from, as no one else in the Glascock family at the time had red hair. And it was bright red!

Noel graduated from Jefferson City High School and went on to earn a bachelor's degree and then a Master's degree from Lincoln University. In the summer of 1980 he began working for the State of Missouri, at the Division of Employment Security. He moved into the research and statistical programs in 1982, and remained in various research capacities with Employment Security, the Division of Workforce Development, and finally the Division of Personnel. Noel retired from the state in August of 2012.

Back during those college years Noel began to spend time with a young lady from Fulton, Missouri. Noel and Deborah Lynn Haymart were married on a bright and warm autumn day on November 8, 1980 on the campus of William Woods University in Fulton. They initially lived just south of Fulton, before eventually moving to Holts Summit.

Noel and Debbie welcomed their first son, Noel Edward Blythe, III, into the world on July 5, 1983. This young boy would, like his grandpa, go by his middle name, Edward. A second son joined the family in 1985, as James Andrew Blythe was born. James shared a birthday with Grandpa Jimmy—December 7th. Somehow, this fact escaped both father and grandmother, as otherwise his middle name probably would have also been Edmund—just like Grandpa Jimmy. Noel and Debbie rounded out their family when Jonathan Ross Blythe was born on November 21st of 1987.

While all three were quite different from each other, all three played ice hockey in Jefferson City, from first grade up through high school. Edward continues as an ice hockey referee in the Kansas City area, while James and Jon look to play adult hockey as often as possible. All three love the ice.

All three boys graduated from Jefferson City High School, before moving out into the world. Edward graduated in 2002, and was the recipient of the school's Art Service Award, despite not taking art classes. He served as the rope crew leader at the annual operetta, which happened to be the Wizard of Oz that year. The operetta included a hot air balloon that actually rose on stage—thanks to the rope crew! Edward joined the Missouri National Guard in 2004, and continues on active duty at the armory in Lexington, Missouri, as a supply sergeant. He married Tammie Lee Houchens from Jefferson City on July 29th, 2006. Tammie was studying Art Education at the University of Central Missouri at Warrensburg and graduated while Edward was overseas, serving a tour in Kosovo. Edward was able to arrange his leave to attend her graduation. Edward and Tammie moved to Independence, Missouri after he returned home, and have two daughters: Estella Rose, born on April 19th, 2009, and Anastasia Alexis, born on April 12th, 2011.

James Andrew graduated in 2004, and attended the Lincoln Technical Institute in Indianapolis, Indiana. Tragically, his fiancée, Whitney Lee Briggs of Hallsville, was killed in a car accident while he was there. He was always gifted with his hands and could handle anything mechanical. James worked for the Gragar Company out of Fulton, Missouri, and now works for the Roadside Repair Company out of St. Louis, Missouri. He resides in Ferguson, Missouri.

Jon graduated in 2006, and then attended Columbia College. He married Tonya Christine Brady, originally from Colorado, on September 8th, 2007. Almost exactly a year later, on September 5th of 2008, Javan Ross Blythe arrived as Noel and Debbie's first grandchild and Ed and Betty's first great-grandchild. They welcomed a second son into the Glascock family when Tiras William Blythe was born on August 16th, 2011. Jon and Tonya and the boys moved to Gladstone, Missouri in August of 2012 where Jon is beginning study at Midwest Baptist Theological Seminary.

Kendall was the tallest member of the Glascock family, reaching an even 6'6" tall. Though he could tower over anyone else, Kendall was the quiet one in the bunch.

Kendall graduated from Jefferson City High in 1977, and also went to Lincoln University, where he earned bachelor's degrees in both Business Administration and Accounting. He married Rhonda Lea Mongler of Columbia on September 11th, of 1983.

Kendall worked as a manager for McDonald's for several years, before also joining the State of Missouri as an auditor in the Department of Economic Development. He went on to work as an auditor for MODOT before becoming the head of internal audits for the Department of Natural Resources.

Kendall and Rhonda have one son, Ross Douglas Blythe, who arrived on December 2nd of 1996. Ross, who may finally challenge his dad as the tallest member of the family, is currently in his sophomore year at Jefferson City High School, where he plays baseball.

Paul is perhaps best known for owning and running the Good Time Country dance hall in Columbia for many years. Paul not only ran the club, but also played bass guitar and did a "little bit" of singing as well. After Paul sold the club, he continued to play in bands until 2011, when he finally retired from playing. Paul also worked for the Columbia School District as a substitute teacher for several years and now works for the Boone Title Company. He has also been active in youth baseball for many years and served as President of the Diamond Council in Columbia for the past decade.

Paul graduated from Jeff City High in 1980 and studied at Lincoln University. He married Cindy Streit of Fulton in 1987. They were divorced in 1992. Paul then married Jody Haden Smarr from Columbia on July 11th, 1993. That union brought not only Jody into the family, but also her two children: Ashley Dawn and Kyle Andrew Smarr. Paul and Jody went on to have another son and a daughter. Joshua Haden Blythe was born April 7th of 1994. Brianne Elizabeth Blythe was born January 7th, 1997.

Both Paul and Jody have worked for many years for Boone Title Company in Columbia. Their daughter Ashley works there as well. Ashley graduated high school in 2005. She married Scott Lee Bain in 2009 (they were divorced in 2012.) Ashley gave Paul and Jody their first two grandchildren. Her daughter, Ava Mckenzie Bain was born in 2009, on May 12th. Her son, Scott Lee Bain, Jr. arrived on July 19th of 2010.

Kyle graduated from Columbia Hickman High School in 2008 and worked in construction for several years. He now works for Midway Arms in Columbia. He is currently in the process of purchasing his first home. Kyle is also a "fitness fanatic" (to quote his dad) and works out on a daily basis. Kyle and his long-time girlfriend, Brittany Sapp, are expecting a son next spring.

Joshua graduated from Columbia Hickman High School in 2012 and began his college life in August of 2012 at the Music Conservatory with the University of Missouri-Kansas City. Josh's high school career was filled with honors, particularly in music. He travelled with the Hickman band to Hawaii, and was then named the All-State Jazz Drummer in the spring of 2012.

Brianne is currently a sophomore at Hickman, but will attend Columbia's new "Muriel Battle High School," next year. Brianne seems intent on breaking at least one gender stereotype, as she is excels at mathematics and is considering pursuing a career in bio-medical engineering. She also plays the flute and bass in school, including the jazz band.

Paul and Jody have also become foster parents, with a new "foster daughter," Brianna LaShea Shelby, who is in the same class with her new foster sister, Brianne. Brianna is on the cross country team at Hickman, and is interested in becoming an ultra-sound technologist.

Betty Jane and Ed celebrated 50 years of marriage in March of 2004. They were honored at a reception at the Truman Hotel in Jefferson City, with a large turnout of friends and family.

Ed passed away on Memorial Day Weekend, May 30th of 2010, at the age of 81, after several years of declining health. He was buried at the Debo Cemetery in Holts Summit, Missouri. Betty Jane continues to live a productive and active life, whether in quilting, in her local church, or in running around with her sisters.

The family line through Ross and Lola has grown to a total 82 direct descendants from Grandpa Jimmy and Grandma Maggie. Ross and Lola would add 5 children, 14 grandchildren, 31 great-grandchildren, and another 31 great-great grandchildren. Add to that number the step-children among the great-grandchildren and great-great-grandchildren, and the family swells to some 95 members. Then add to that the spouses of the descendants (another thirty-five) and the legacy of the family Ross and Lola makes for a 131 members, of which 121 remain alive as of the 100th Anniversary Reunion.

CHAPTER TEN:

The Family of Clarice & Oren Wren

After four sons, James and Margaret added their first daughter to their family. Clarice Emma was born on July 31, 1900. It was a new century and progress and tragedy marked the year. Kodak would introduce the "Brownie" Camera, which was the first hand-held camera easy enough so that even a child could use it. It would cost one dollar. The Presidential campaign would see William McKinley re-elected. On September the 1st, thousands of Americans would die when the city of Galveston was nearly obliterated by a hurricane. And the decennial census showed that the American population had grown by over 21% since 1890.

Clarice, as did her brothers and sister, grew up on the farm in the Wilton area. Life on the farm for girls was similar in many respects to that of their brothers. Girls were certainly expected to do their share of the chores. Those chores though, tended to be more near the house than out in the fields. Chores such as churning butter or helping with canning vegetables often fell to the girls of the house. Life entailed plenty of hard work, but had its rewards as well.

The formal education of any of Grandpa Jimmy's and Grandma Maggie's children meant progressing through the eighth grade. The realities of farm life in rural mid-America simply dictated that there would be little opportunity for the vast majority of children to go further in school. Like her brothers and sisters, Clarice would have not travelled too far from home in those early years.

As young Clarice grew into a young lady, a certain man had been catching her eye for several years. Oren Preller Wren became the object of her heart and she of his too! But the First World War intervened. Oren was drafted into the U.S. Army in the autumn of 1918. He went through boot camp and was on the boat, ready to go to Europe when word came that an Armistice had been reached and the war was over. Oren was back in Boone County within a few weeks, and Clarice married her sweetheart on March 16th, 1919.

The couple was married in the bride's home. This was often customary in those years. Oren's family did not attend the wedding because, as was also customary, the groom's family typically did not attend. If they did it was seen as a sign they were too anxious to get their son "married off," or they were expressing false pride. So Clarice and Oren spent their wedding day and night in the home of Jimmy and Maggie, before going to Oren's home.

Oren had spent the day of the wedding taking the train from Wilton up to Columbia. He took an empty suitcase for the suit he intended to buy. When he got there he found that his sister Leora and Aunt Mamie had hidden two big corncobs in the suitcase. Oren had to duck out into a back alley, dispose of the cobs, and then pack his suit.

Clarice was married in a dress she made with the help of her sister-in-law, Stella. It was pure silk crepe de Chine, white with a Peter Pan collar, long sleeves, open down front, with lace on the collar and side of the cuffs.

The story is told that the wedding cake came out of the oven that afternoon with a crack across the top. Her mother told her that was a sign that their first child would be a girl.

The ceremony was performed by Elder F. F. Querry of Goshen Church. As the wedding party gathered, Elder Querry went through the ceremony so quickly that Grandma Maggie was barely in the room when he pronounced Oren and Clarice husband and wife.

Oren and Clarice setup house in a log cabin in the area of Easley and Nashville. Oren worked for the railroad through those early years, which afforded the family few opportunity to ride the train up to Columbia for free in order to visit family.

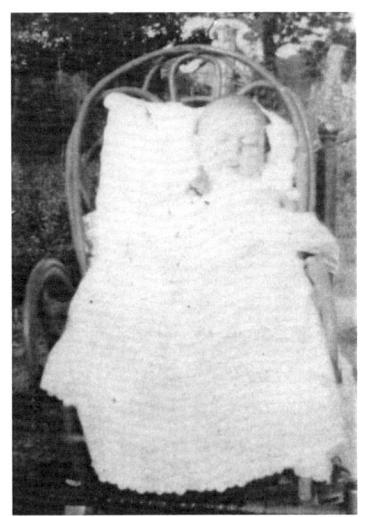 In the spring of 1920, on the 17th of May, Amy Ester (often called Janie) Wren arrived as their first child. The family moved quite often. The first son, Virgil Oren, born August 24th, 1921, was also born in the Easley-Nashville area, but in a different home. They then moved onto a farm on Smith Hatchery Road above Easley.

 A second son, Lahmon Emery was born there, on the 31st of March in 1923. By the next year they moved to Wilton, at the corner of Route M and Cedar Tree Lane. Thurman Sterling (usually called "Tommy") was born there, on December 5th, 1924. He was their third son.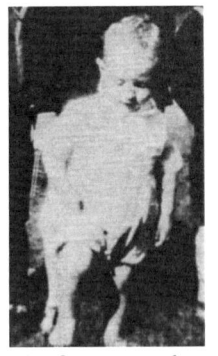

Now with three sons and the one daughter, it would be nearly eight years before another baby came into the family of Clarice and Oren. During this time Oren left the railroad and farmed in the river bottom around Wilton. They lived in the river bottom for a few years, and then moved near both the Old William Wren School, and the New William Wren School.

 Emma Fern was born there, on July 8th, 1932.

During the depths of the Great Depression, Oren went to work on the dam east of Ashland for a couple of years, and then worked on a W.P.A. project in Rolla, Missouri during 1938 and 1939. Later in life, during the 1950's and 1960's, Oren worked on the grounds of Stephens College in Columbia. He retired from the college.

With their growing family they moved near Easley, and then in 1935, they moved into a home on Cedar Tree Lane. They would stay in this home until they moved into Ashland in 1977. Two more daughters arrived once they settled on Cedar Tree Lane.

Oleta Chloe was born on February 20th, 1936 and Lora Ann arrived on the 22nd of June in 1938. The Wren family now numbered four girls and three boys. The age spread of the family was a little larger than many of the rest of the Glascock families. Esther, the oldest, was a young woman of eighteen, nearly ready to leave the nest, while the youngest was the baby, Lora Ann, who had just arrived.

Before the older ones left the nest to start their own families, the Second World War intervened on their generation just as the First World War had intervened on their parents. Virgil, Lahmon and Thurman all served during the war, from Europe to the Pacific. And just as the sons of the family had always gone off to serve their country, the daughters waited at home for husbands and husbands-to-be to return.

Esther married Will Harney Lewis on June 14th, 1943. Bill served in the U.S. Navy during the war. Virgil also married while in the service, as he and Virginia Louise Crump were married on October 26th, 1944.

After the war, the family began to grow quickly. Lahmon married Mary Lee Bennett on June 28th, 1945. Thurman returned home and was wedded to Fonda Graham on the 29th of December of 1953.

The service of her sons during the war led Clarice to be very active in the American War Mothers organization later in life. She held several local and state offices for many years, and travelled across Missouri every year for the state convention. She would also work a day a week as a volunteer at the VA Hospital in Columbia.

The Wren family was also devoted Cardinal baseball fans. Radio brought the games into homes all across Missouri every day. Even in his later years, Oren, who might have seemed to be dozing off during a game, knew the score if asked!

It was during this time that Grandpa Jimmy lived with Clarice and Oren. When Grandma Maggie died, Lahmon went to live with his grandpa for a few weeks, while Ross and Lola moved in with him. When Ross was appointed as postmaster in Hartsburg and he and Lola moved there, Jimmy moved in with Clarice and Oren. Having Grandpa Jimmy in the home meant some accommodations had to be made. The younger girls remember his fussing about the radio at night. He always wanted to hear all the news (a habit he developed during the war) and since the radios ran on batteries, he would fuss if anyone else used the radio and used up the batteries! In his final years Grandpa Jimmy was a semi-invalid and someone would have to stay with him no matter what the family occasion might be.

Grandchildren for Clarice and Oren were also beginning to arrive. Their first was a grandson, Roxie Dale Lewis, the eldest son of Esther and Bill. Dale was born on

February 9th, 1944.   His younger brother, William Troy Lewis, arrived on October 10 1946.   The next year, 1947, saw the arrival of two more grandchildren.   Their first granddaughter, Alvera Wren, arrived on February 19th to her proud parents, Virgil and Virginia.   Another granddaughter was born to Lahmon and Mary Lee on the 26th of August, named Linda Gayle Wren.

The year 1951 brought the next set of new children in the family of Clarice and Oren. Deborah Kay Wren was born to Lahmon and Mary Lee on March 11th, while Virgil and Virginia welcomed Brent Wren on October 22nd.

In later years, during the 1950's, Clarice worked in a clothing factory in Jefferson City, and then for the Sudden Service Cleaners in Columbia mending clothes.

By now, the younger girls were beginning to leave the family home, marry, and begin homes of their own.   Oleta married Joseph Benton Forsee on September 12th, of 1954. Emma Fern married William Perry McDonald on August 8th of 1958.   And just a month later, Lora Ann was married with Donald Eugene Jones on the 20th of September of 1958. With all the children married, the family began to grow even more rapidly.

Gregory Kent Wren was the next grandson to arrive, on July 24th, 1954.   He would be the first son to Lahmon and Mary Lee.   A second son was not long in following, as Terry Duane Wren arrived on December 17th, 1956.   In the meantime, Virgil and Virginia added another grandson to the family, with the birth of Roland Dean Wren on March 25th, 1955.

Thurman and Fonda began their family with the birth of Carolyn Sue Wren on the 2nd of May, 1955.   Unfortunately the baby survived only a day.   The couple then welcomed their first son a year later, on June 12th, 1956, with the birth of Larry Graham Wren.

Oleta and Joe began their family as well with the arrival of two sons.   David Oren Forsee was born on May 20th, 1956, while younger brother Michael Lee Forsee arrived on July

3, 1957. The decade closed out with the arrival of two more granddaughters. Cynthia Kay Wren was born into the family of Thurman and Fonda, on March 6th, 1959. Virgil and Virginia welcomed another daughter, Karla Louise Wren, on August 10th, 1959.

The new decade did not slow the growth in the family at all. Thurman and Fonda completed their family with the arrival of Charlene Denise Wren on May 27th, of 1960. Oleta and Joe added another daughter to the family with the birth of Rebecca Gay Forsee on December 7th, 1960. Perry and Emma Fern began their family with the birth of their son, Randall Perry McDonald, on May 3rd, 1960. A year later they welcomed twin daughters, born on March 9th, 1961, named Gayle Marie and Gwyn Ann McDonald.

Lora Ann and Donald began their family late in 1962, with the arrival of Mark Eugene Jones on the 23rd of December. Oleta and Joe then completed their family with the birth of Elizabeth Kay Forsee on February 18th, 1963. Traci Dawn Wren arrived on August 2nd, 1963 to complete Lahmon's and Mary Lee's family. A second son was born to Lora and Donald on May 12th, 1964, when Lyle Curtis Jones arrived.

Clarice and Oren had three more granddaughters who arrived in the late 1960's and early 1970's. Lisa Lynn McDonald, daughter of Emma Fern and Perry, was born on June 16th

in 1967. Angela Mae Wren was welcomed into the family of Virgil and Virginia on September 17th, 1968. Their last grandchild, a daughter by Lora and Donald, arrived on June 17th, 1974, with the birth of Susan Elizabeth Jones.

March 19th, 1969, marked the golden anniversary of Oren and Clarice's wedding. Friends and family gathered at Woodcrest Church in Ashland to celebrate. They had hoped to have the reception at Goshen where they attended, but the weather that March made that problematic. Goshen Hill could become nearly impassible during snow and ice storms. And sure enough, a late winter storm hit the day before!

Oren and Clarice, along with all of their children, gathered on Saturday night at Oscar's Steak House down in Jefferson City for a family meal. Thurman's family, who were travelling from Wichita, Kansas, arrived just in time. They then gathered at Esther's home to visit for a while.

Overnight, the temperature dropped below freezing and froze the ginger ale for the punch that Lora Ann had in the trunk of her car. Each bottle burst and ginger ale was all over the trunk. Fortunately the Whitfield's, who owned a grocery store in Ashland, managed to get them enough ginger ale for the reception. Keep in mind that this was still during the time of blue laws, and most stores were closed on Sundays.

Some of the grandchildren sang a song about their grandparents. Clarice also wore a pin that day that her mother, Maggie, had worn at her fiftieth wedding anniversary. Maggie's mother, Matilda Rippeto, had given her that pin and it was now being passed down. The pin has since been worn by Oleta, Fern and Lora at their fiftieth anniversary celebrations.

Oren and Clarice would celebrate their wedding together for many years afterwards. In fact, they would celebrate 69 years of marriage in March of 1988.

In their 69th year together, Clarice was diagnosed with a malignant tumor on one of her kidneys. The kidney and tumor were removed, but the doctors only gave her a couple of months to live. And that was about the length of time she had left. Clarice passed away on October 22nd, 1988. Oren survived for a couple of more years, but the loss of his wife was hard and he spent most of that time in the VA nursing home. He departed this world on January 22nd, 1991.

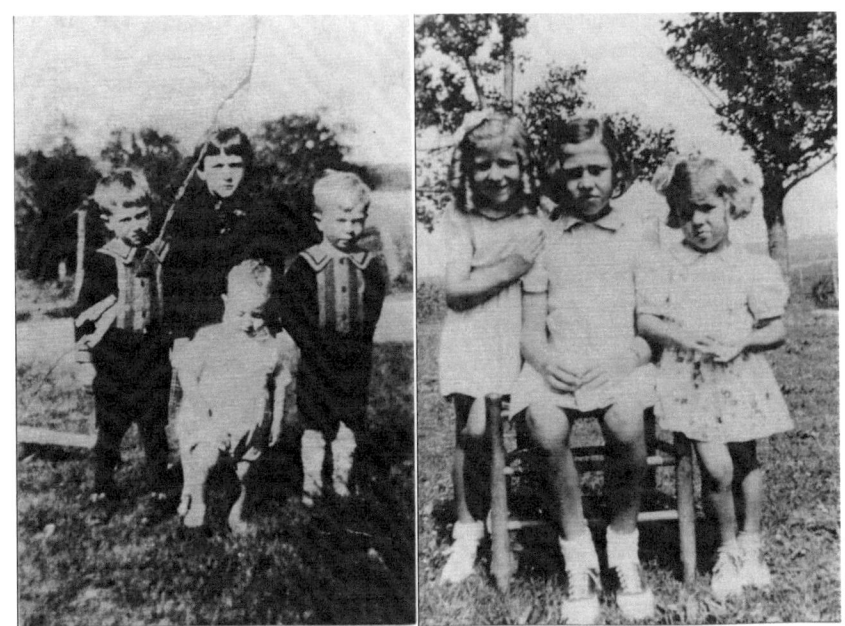

THE FAMILY OF ESTHER & BILL

Esther was Oren and Clarice's first child, born May 17th, 1920. Esther graduated from high school and moved to Kansas City to work.

A couple of years later, she moved across the state to work in St. Louis. She met a young man named Bill Lewis, and they were married on June 14th, 1943. Bill left for the war shortly thereafter, and Esther moved back to Ashland and started teaching school. She went to the University of Missouri for a couple of years, and then transferred to Lincoln University in Jefferson City to complete her degree in education in 1968. She taught elementary school for some 36 years—the first 23 years at Ashland, before she moved to Vandalia, Missouri, to teach another 13 years. From there she retired, moved back to Ashland, and did substitute teaching. By the time her career was complete, she had taught the parents, children, and in some cases grandchildren of families in Ashland.

Esther and Bill raised two sons along the way. Roxie Dale Lewis was born on February 9th, 1944, while Bill was still in the service. A second son, William Troy (usually went by Troy) Lewis arrived in 1946, on October 10th of that year.

Dale married Darlene (Dolly) Beck on May 28th, 1966. Their daughter, Shelly Roxanne Lewis, arrived on June 28th, 1970. Their son, William (Bill) Floyd Lewis, was born on May 9th, 1975. After returning home from the Navy, Dale made a career in the telephone business, working for GTE, Verizon, and Century Tel.

Shelly married Scott Long on the 8th of July in 1989. Their daughter was born on June 10th, 1992. She was named Darcy Jane Long. Their oldest son, Jesse Garron Long, was born on April 28th, 1994. Their third child, a son named Jacob Scott Long, arrived on July 10th, 1997.

Bill married Hope Walbrecht on June 10th, 1995. They would welcome three daughters into the family. Myah Gail Lewis was born on April 1st, 1999. Kaylie Paige Lewis arrived on June 13th, 2000. A third daughter, Faith Ann Lewis, was born on March 2nd, 2003. Bill and Hope were subsequently divorced. Bill and Tammy Schmidt have a set of twin sons. Liem Morgan Lewis and William Murphy Lewis both arrived on December 6th, 2011.

Troy married Janice Sapp on June 24th, 1966. They had two daughters. Amy Louise Lewis was born on January 9th, 1967. Elizabeth Ann Lewis arrived on May 18th, 1972. Troy and Janice were then divorced, and he then married Nellie Connell in May of 1981. Their union would produce a son, Adam Lee Lewis, who was born on September 8th, 1982. Troy worked in the plumbing business in Columbia and Boone County until his retirement. He and Nellie are now divorced and Troy currently lives in Centralia.

Amy Louise married Dan Amundson on the 4th of March, 1990. They welcomed a daughter and then a son into the family. Taylor Leigh Amundson was born January 18th,

1995. Code Clay Amundson arrived on August 2nd, 1997. Dan passed away on August 7th, 2009.

Elizabeth Ann married Steve Hale on July 6th, 2001. Their oldest son, Douglas Alexandra Hale, was born on December 8th, 1999. A second boy, Conner Dane Hale, arrived on June 7th, 2001.

Adam Lee married Candida Marcum on the 18th of September, 2004.

Bill Lewis passed away on his 55th birthday—February 10th, 1964. He was buried at the New Salem Cemetery in Ashland. Esther remains as the senior living member of the family of Jimmy and Maggie Glascock.

THE FAMILY OF VIRGIL & VIRGINIA

Virgil was the first son and second child of Clarice and Oren, born August 24th, 1921. As a young man of twenty-one years of age, Virgil found himself in the U.S. Army-Air Force, eventually fighting in Europe.

While home on leave, he married Virginia Crump on October 25, 1944.

In 1946, when Virgil returned home from the war, he and Virginia lived in Columbia where he worked for Missouri Motors. They eventually moved to Ashland where he managed a Phillips 66 service station. He then went into business with this brother-in-law, Bill Lewis, and they owned and operated the school bus company for the Ashland School District for many years. That meant driving for many late night trips for the school's athletic teams! In his later years he worked for the Boone County Water District up until his death in 1990.

Virgil and his brother Lahmon (along with many others in the family!) played a lot of baseball through the adult lives. Town baseball was a big event during those years, and they played in Ashland and Hartsburg until they finally were too old to play with the younger players any more. This one love that runs throughout the Wren family to this day!

Virgil and Virginia brought five children into this world—three daughters and two sons. The oldest child was Alvera Wren, who arrived on February 19th, 1947. She was followed by her two brothers. Brent Wren was born on October 22nd, of 1951, while younger brother Roland Dean Wren was welcomed into the family on March 25th, 1955. Karla Louise Wren was born some four years later, in 1959, on the 10th of August. The youngest of the family, Angela Mae Wren, was then some nine years in arriving! She was born in September of 1968, on the 17th of the month.

Alvera married Walter Bernard Doerge on September 20th, 1968. Their son, Brain Keith, was born on April 28th, 1969. Their daughter, Jennifer Marie Doerge, arrived on September 20th, 1982. Alvera worked for several years for the University of Missouri, and now works for the Boyce Bynum Laboratory in Columbia. Alvera and her husband currently live in Hallsville.

Brian married Stacy Holzinger on August 2nd, 1991. They made Alvera and Walter grandparents with the birth of Kameron Walter Xavier Doerge on September 10th, 1991.

Jennifer was married with Tim Ortman on July 28th, 2001. Their famiy currently consists of a daughter, Evelyn Prayse Ortman, who arrived on July 18th, 2002, and a son, Josiah James Ortman, who was born on January 23rd, 2006.

Brent Wren served in the military, and did a tour in Vietnam. He added a daughter to the family, Sara Lee-Anne Wren, who was born on October 11th, 1994. He currently lives and works in the Moberly area.

Roland Dean married Paula Perkins on April 12th, 1974. Their union produced two daughters. Emily Nicole Wren was born on September 22nd, 1983. Younger sister Ashley Dawn Wren was born on April 6th of 1985. Roland worked for many years on the Boone County Transportation road crew. He and Paula live in Ashland on Virgil and Virginia's home place.

Emily Nicole married Michael Hanafusa on May 10th, 2008. They currently have a son, Brayden Michael Hanafusa, born April 28th, 2010.

Karla Louise married Denis Lenger on December 23rd, 1977. Kristina Louise Lenger, their oldest daughter, was born on May 5th, 1983. Their son, Derek William Lenger, arrived on November 25th, 1986. A second daughter, Kelcie Laura Lenger, was born on the 8th of June in 1989. Karla works as a Fiscal Assistant for the U.S. Department of Agriculture's Conservation Services. Karla is currently divorced and lives in Ashland.

Kristina Louise married Mark Branch on September 24th, 2005. They currently have a son, Mason Kane Branch, born on February 4th, 2009.

Derek married Sheila Campbell on April 17th, 2009. They also currently have a daughter, Charli Jo Lenger, born on December 18th, 2009.

Angela Mae married Kyle George on the 16th of July in 1988. They would have a son and a daughter to add to the family. Benjamin Linwood Wren George was born on April 8th, 1990. Morgan Elaine George arrived on October 25th, 1993. Angela and Kyle live in Hallsville. Angie has worked many years at the University of Missouri, and is currently an Administrative Assistant in the Department Animal Science. Virgil died on March 7th, 1990 and was laid to rest in Goshen Cemetery

THE FAMILY OF LAHMON & MARY LEE

Lahmon Emery was the third in the family of Clarice and Oren, arriving March 31st in 1923. He followed his older brother, Virgil, into World War II, being inducted on February 11th, 1943. He served in both the European and Pacific theaters of the war, and was part of the occupation force in Japan.

Lahmon and Mary Lee Bennett were married on June 28th, 1945, while Lahmon was on leave. When he returned home from the war, he went to work as a mechanic for Missouri Motors in Columbia. He then opened his own garage in Ashland, known as "Wren's Garage." He owned and operated the business for some fifty years, before turning it over to his son, Terry, and his grandson, Derek, which has kept the business in the family. Lahmon also served as Mayor of Ashland and was a founding member of the Ashland Optimist Club. After he retired, Lahmon took up golf, a game he grew to love until this death.

Lahmon and Mary Lee also had five children, and, like his older brother, had three girls and two boys. Linda Gayle Wren was the oldest, born on the 26th of August in 1947. Nearly four years later, they welcomed their second daughter, Deborah Kay Wren, in the family on March 11th, 1951. Two sons followed, with the birth of Gregory Kent Wren on July 24th, 1954, and the birth of Terry Duane Wren on December 17th, 1956. Their family was complete with the arrival of their third daughter nearly seven years later. Traci Dawn Wren was born on the 2nd of August in 1963.

Linda Gayle attended the University of Missouri-Kansas City. She married Jerry Arnold on March 11th, 1965. They had one daughter, Leslie Suzanne Arnold, born on the 10th of February in 1966. Their son, Bryce Jefferson Arnold, arrived on January 6th, 1975. Linda worked as Vice President of Human Resources for the Toastmaster Corporation for 28 years before retiring. She now works as the Senior Vice-President for Human Resources for the Landmark Bank Company. Linda is currently divorced and lives in Ashland.

Leslie was wed with Dan Siegfried on March 17th, 1990. They welcomed two daughters into the family. Jordyn Taylor Siegfried arrived on December 20th, 1993. Hunter Leigh Siegfried was born on May 27th, 1998.

Bryce married Melody Rouse on the 24th of April in 2004. They had twin sons born on November 25th, 2006: Payton Jefferson Arnold and Emery Leland Arnold.

Deborah Kay (Deb) married Jim Bowden on October 19th, 1968. Their family consisted of a son and a daughter. Their son, Christopher Sean Bowden, arrived on February 15th, 1969. Heather Nicole Bowden, their daughter, was born on January 15th, 1975. Deb and Jim still live in Ashland. Deb made a career with the University of Missouri for some 33 years, working as an Executive Staff Assistant in the Department of Surgery and then the Department of Obstetrics.

Christopher married Christy Nichols in 1990, on the 30th of June. Their first child was a son, Brandon Lee Bowden, born on December 7th, 1985. The oldest daughter, Lindsey Dawn Bowden, arrived on February 7th, 1987. A second daughter, Megan Renae Bowden, was born on the 26th of January of 1988. They completed their family with the birth of Danielle Nicole Bowden on August 27th, 1991.

Both Megan and Danielle have made grandparents of Debbie and Jim. Megan and Devin Craig welcomed a daughter with the birth of Kamdyn Elizabeth Craig on November 24th, 2009. Danielle and Victor Gregori have two daughters, Delaney Shae Gregori, born August 17th, 2011, and younger sister, Kinley Elyse Gregori, born this past August, on the 20th, in 2012.

Heather Nicole Married William Nichols on July 10th, 1999. They have one son, Adyn Patrick Nichols, who arrived on January 28th, 2006.

Gregory Kent attended Northeast Missouri State University and earned a bachelor's degree in Business. He went into the banking business, working at various banks in both Columbia and Jefferson City. He currently is with Central Trust Bank in Jefferson City.

Terry went to Lincoln University on a baseball scholarship. He and Peggy Hulen were married on March 20th, 1976. Derek Neal Wren was born on August 20th, 1976. They had a second son, Damon Cole Wren, who arrived on June 10th, 1981. Terry started working the garage with his dad, and continued there until he and Peggy took over the garage in 1995. He still runs the family business—Wren's Garage—now with the help of his son, Derek.

Derek married Lisa Bartow on April 10th, 1999. Their oldest daughter, Jayden Lynae Wren was born on May 17th, 2000. Derek and Lisa's second daughter, Riley Dalene

Wren, was unfortunately stillborn on June 8th, 2002. A third daughter, Jersee Ryelle Wren, arrived on September 2nd, 2003. Derek and Lisa rounded out their family with a son, Jace Neal Wren, born on the 19th of July in 2006. Derek continues working with his father in Wren's Garage in Ashland.

Damon was married to Sarah Gill on May 14th, 2005. They currently have two daughters, Adison Dalene Wren, born on June 2nd, 2007, and Drew Taylor Wren, who arrived on February 10th, 2009. They recently added a son to their family, with the birth of Drake Christian Wren on December 28th, 2011.

Traci attended Northeast Missouri State University and worked in patient accounts at the University of Missouri Hospital. She married Michael Howard on the first day of July in 1995, and moved to South Carolina where Michael was stationed in the U.S. Marine Corps. Michael made a career in the U.S. military. They have two sons, Brennan Rhyse Howard, born on December 2nd, 1997, and Brayden Ren Howard, who arrived on February 22nd, 1999. After Michael's retirement, they have returned to Ashland where Traci now works as an administrator for the Boone Hospital Center.

Lahmon and Mary Lee were honored for their Golden Anniversary in 1995. They celebrated with an open house reception at the Optimist Building in Ashland.

Lahmon passed away on October 8th, 2007. He is buried in New Salem Cemetery in Ashland.

THE FAMILY OF THURMAN & FONDA

Thurman was the third and final son of Clarice and Oren, arriving on December 5th, 1924. He grew up on the farm and, like his brothers, went off to fight in the Second World War. Thurman joined the U.S. Navy on April 24th, 1944, and spent the war aboard an oiler during the last year of the Pacific Campaign.

When Thurman returned home he began attending the University of Missouri. After graduation, he went to work as a County Extension Agent in Columbus, Kansas. While attending a conference in Denver, Colorado, one year, he met Fonda Graham, who was from Texas. Before long Thurman and Fonda were married and living in Kansas. Thurman then took a position in Wichita, Kansas.

Thurman and Fonda began their family with the birth of a daughter, Carolyn Sue, on May 2nd, 1955. She lived only a day however. By the next June they welcomed their first son into the family, when Larry Graham Wren was born on the 12th of June, 1956. Two more daughters followed. Cynthia Kay Wren arrived on March 6th, 1959, and the youngest, Charlene Denise Wren, was born on May 27th, 1960.

Larry married Melinda Morgan on June 28th, 1980. Their family would grow with the arrival of two sons. Jonathan Morgan Wren was born on July 19th, 1981. Joel Graham Wren arrived the last day of the year—December 31st—in 1984. Larry graduated from Manhattan Christian College with a B.S. in Christian Education. He went on to earn a Master of Arts degree from Friends University in Wichita, Kansas. He now serves as executive pastor at Pathway Christian Church in Wichita.

Cynthia went to Kansas State University after high school, and earned a bachelor's degree in Family Economics. She worked many years for the Kansas Electric Company, and currently works in the Wichita Public Schools. She married Russell Van Pelt on June 5th, 1981. They had two daughters. Elizabeth Denise Van Pelt was born on August 11th, 1987. Younger sister Emily Kathleen Van Pelt arrived on April 26nd, 1989. Russell passed away on 1st of May, 2003, at the age of 44. Both Cynthia and Russell's girls are now married. Both wed in the year 2011. Elizabeth married Ryan C. Noble on September 24th, while Emily married Chris Keyser on June 3rd.

Charlene Denise went to Kansas State University and attained a B.S. degree in Education. She also attended Manhattan Christian College and earned a B.S. in Christian Education. She went on to earn a Master's degree in Educational Leadership from Wichita State University. She has spent her career in the Wichita Public School District in Kansas, working as a Principal and as an Assistant Superintendent. She currently is the Director of Leadership Development for the AVID Center in San Diego, California. She continues to reside in the Wichita area.

Thurman passed away on the 18th of February in 1970, at the age of 45 years. Fonda followed him in death on November 18th, 2009. They lay at rest today, side by side, in Jamesburg Park Cemetery in Wichita, Kansas.

THE FAMILY OF EMMA FERN & PERRY

It was nearly eight years since the birth of Thurman before Clarice and Oren added their next child. Emma Fern Wren was born on the 8th of July, 1932. After high school, Emma Fern moved to Columbia and work at several jobs, including in the Boone County Clerk's Office.

She married William Perry McDonald in August of 1958. They moved to Caruthersville, Missouri. Perry was an accountant, and Emma Fern helped out in his business when she was not busy with the children at home.

Fern and Perry welcomed their first child into their new family on May 3rd, 1960, when Randall (Randy) Perry McDonald was born. The next year they had twin girls— Gayle Marie McDonald and Gwyn Ann McDonald, both born on March 9th, of 1961. They rounded out their family in 1967 when Lisa Lynn McDonald arrived on the 16th of June.

Randy went to Harding College in Searcy, Arkansas and earned a degree in Business and Accounting. He would work in the family accounting business until the time of his death. He married Sherra Colvett on August 25th, 1990. They would have one son, Ben Randall McDonald, born October 23rd, 1991. Randy though did not live to meet his son. Randy became a volunteer fireman in the Caruthersville Fire Department. On a Friday afternoon, March 8th, in 1991, a major fire broke out in downtown Caruthersville. At the peak of the fire, the north outer wall of a two-story building collapsed onto Randy. Though he was pulled from the debris within moments, the crush of brick and debris had already killed him. In honor of his sacrifice his badge number was permanently retired by the Caruthersville Fire Department, and the newest fire truck in their force was dedicated in his memory. Randy was laid to rest in his hometown of Caruthersville, Missouri.

Gwyn Ann went to Freed Hardiman University and attained her associate's degree there. She married Doug McDowell on August 15th, 1980. They had a son and a daughter. Adam Douglas McDowell was born on July 20th, 1985. Sara Clarise McDowell arrived on the 5th of June, 1987. Both have since married. Adam wed Susan Boyette on June 14th, 2008. Sara was married with Richard Wood on May 23rd, 2008. Gwyn and Doug raised their family in the Caruthersville area, where Gwyn worked in the public school system and in the family accounting business as well.

Gayle Marie went to Freed Hardiman University in Tennessee and earned a bachelor's degree there. She went on to receive a master's degree from Memphis State University. She has worked for many years as an athletic trainer at the University of Memphis and is an instructor at Freed Hardiman University in Tennessee.

Lisa Lynn attended St. Mary's College in St. Louis, Missouri, and earned a B.S. in Nursing. Lisa and Scotty Al Sup were married on the 10th of August in 1990. They added two sons to the family. Logan Matthew Al Sup was born on December 2nd, 1987. Spencer William Al Sup arrived on April 28th, 1998. Lisa and Scotty were divorced and Lisa remarried. She and Jamie Gore were wed on October 4th, 2008. Lisa is a registered nurse and has worked in the ER during most of her career. She currently works in a hospital in Blytheville, Arkansas. She and Jamie live in Caruthersville, Missouri.

Through their later years, Fern and Perry loved to go "antiquing" and collecting. Fern has collected many dishes over the years. Perry collects both railroad locks and National Geographic magazines. He has an extensive collection of both!

Emma Fern and Perry celebrated fifty years of marriage in 2008. Friends and family joined them at an open house reception at the Church of Christ in Caruthersville in their honor.

Perry passed away on the first day of November in 2011. He is buried in the Prairie Cemetery in Caruthersville, Missouri.

THE FAMILY OF OLETA & JOE

Oleta Chloe was the third daughter of Clarice and Oren, born February 20th, 1936, in the house on Cedar Tree Lane. Oleta attended the University of Missouri—at least until she met a young man named Joe Forsee!

Joe and Oleta were married on September 12th, 1954. Joe was in the newspaper business and worked at the Columbia Tribune as circulation manager. His work would take them all over the state of Missouri—to Sedalia, St. Joseph, St. Louis and eventually back to Columbia. Oleta worked as a secretary during this time.

In 1980 Joe took a position as the Director of the International Circulation Manager Association in Reston, Virginia. Oleta worked in the office with Joe during this time, being his "right hand girl." This also afforded Oleta and Joe the chance to travel across the United States and aboard. During one memorable visit to Europe, they visited Normandy in France, to the same beaches where Joe had landed back in World War II. They lived in Virginia for thirteen years before Joe retired and they moved back to Ashland. Oleta worked for several years after that for the University of Missouri before she retired.

Oleta and Joe raised a family of two sons and two daughters. David Oren Forsee was born on March 20th, 1956. His younger brother, Michael Lee Forsee, arrived on July 3rd of 1957. The oldest daughter, Rebecca Gay Forsee, was born December 7th, 1960. They rounded out their family with the birth of Elizabeth Kay Forsee on February 18th, 1963.

David went to the University of Missouri and earned a B.S. in Business and Accounting. David also earned his CPA and CMA licenses and has worked as the comptroller for a manufacturing firm in St. Louis for many years.

He married Lisa Duke in January of 1975. Their son, Joseph Lloyd Forsee, was born on April 22nd, 1975. David and Lisa were divorced afterwards, and David remarried. He and Beth O'Brian were wed on September 15th, 1984. They added two sons and a daughter to the family. Brain Michael Foresee was born on January 4th of 1989. Margaret Mary Forsee arrived on the 29th of December in 1990. Their third child, Peter William Forsee, was born on December 8th, 1993. Peter is currently playing baseball at Coker College in South Carolina. David and Beth currently live in Webster Groves, Missouri.

Joseph followed both his father and his grandfather in attending and graduating from the University of Missouri. He was also the first of Oleta and Joe's grandchildren to marry. He married Jody Bucher on September 30th, 2000. On May 11th, 2004, Oleta and Joe became great-grandparents with the arrival of Emma Margaret Forsee. Chloe Genevieve Forsee followed her older sister when she was born on January 31st, 2007. Oleta and Joe's first great-grandson arrived on June 2nd, 2010, with the birth of Jacob David Forsee.

Michael earned a bachelor's degree from the University of Missouri, and then an MBA from the University of Denver. He was married with Terin Cullen on March 20th, 1992. Two years later, in 1994, their son, James Benton Forsee, was born on the 25th of August. A daughter followed in 1996, when Kaitlyn Nicole Forsee was born on July 4th–an Independence Day baby! They make their home in the Denver area, where Michael works with the Denver Telephone Company and IBM.

Rebecca attended Southwest Baptist College and the University of Missouri. She married Randy Jones on May 21st, 1984. Their family consists of a son and a daughter. Their son, Kevin Randall Jones, was born on the 10th of January, 1989. Their daughter,

Mary Elizabeth Jones, arrived on September 19th, 1990. Rebecca and Randy have been subsequently divorced. Rebecca continues to live in Washington, D.C., where she works as a desktop publisher, working with government contracts in our nation's capitol.

When Oleta and Joe moved back to Ashland, their daughter, Elizabeth Kay, remained in Virginia, where she graduated from George Mason University with a bachelor's degree. She went on to earn her MBA from American University in Washington, D.C. She is the departmental senior accountant with a large government contractor in Washington.

Oleta and Joe celebrated their Golden Anniversary with a trip to Washington D.C. with all their family in 1994.

THE FAMILY OF LORA ANN & DON

The seventh and last child of Clarice and Oren was a girl—Lora Ann Wren--born June 22nd, 1938. Like her older sister Oleta, she mostly grew up in the house on Cedar Tree Lane. After high school, Lora Ann attended Stephens College in Columbia for a year, while working at the House Beautiful Beauty Salon as an apprentice hair dresser. She worked as a hair dresser for several years, until she become a stay-at-home mom.

She met Donald Eugene Jones, and they were married on September 20th, 1958.

Don worked as a school administrator for some thirty years, and they lived in several different areas in Missouri. They spent 8 years in the Ashland School District, and another 17 years in the Wright City School District. Once her children were in school, Lora Ann worked as a teacher's aide. Don retired and they moved back to Ashland. Lora Ann went to work at the University of Missouri's College of Education, before retiring after 14 years of service.

Lora Ann also played the piano and the organ, and continues playing organ at Goshen Church, as she has for many years. Lora and Don also travel extensively, often with her older sister, Oleta, and her husband, Joe.

Lora Ann and Don would have a family of two sons and a daughter. Mark Eugene Jones was born on December 23rd, 1962. Younger brother Lyle Curtis Jones came along on the 12th of May in 1964. Their daughter, Susan Elizabeth Jones, arrived in 1974—a decade after her brothers. She was born on June 17th of that year.

Mark went to Kansas State University and attained a bachelor's degree in Business. He then came back to the University of Missouri Law School. After graduating, he worked in Kansas City as an attorney for several years. He is currently Director of Litigation at Shelter Insurance in Columbia.

Mark married Kimberly Sachs on April 24th, 1993. Mark and Kim live and raised their family in the Ashland area. They have a son, Samuel Preller Jones, who arrived on Independence Day—the 4th of July—in 1994. Their first daughter, Madeleine Louise Jones, was born on the 24th of January, 1996. They completed their family with the arrival of Clarice Kay Jones on October 22nd, 1997. Samuel continues with the family's love of baseball. As a left-handed pitcher, he is currently entertaining several scholarship offers for college.

Lyle went to Truman State University in Kirksville, Missouri, and earned a B.S. in Design Technology. He married Shelley Simpson in 1988, on the 6th of August. They have two daughters, Paige Danielle Jones, who arrived on September 30th, 1992, and Kylie Ann Jones, born on May 20th, 1996. Lyle and Shelley live in the Wentzville, Missouri area, where Lyle works as a project manager and supervisor of trim carpenters for a construction company.

Susan attended Southwest Missouri State University and the University of Missouri after high school. She graduated with a B.S. in Occupational Therapy. She would marry Cory Blackburn on September 27th, 1997. They also have lived in Ashland through their married lives. Their union would add two more sons to the family. Ethan Harris Blackburn arrived on May 4th, 2000. Younger brother Gavin Clark Blackburn was born on December 5th, 2003. Susan works as an occupational therapist for the Southern Boone County School District.

Lora and Don celebrated their Golden Anniversary in 2008. They were honored at an open house reception with family and friends, and then gathered for a dinner with their family and closest friends at the Optimist Building in Ashland.

Clarice and Oren began a family which grew rapidly. They would have 7 children, who would, in turn, give them 27 grandchildren. They would then add 47 great-grandchildren. The next generation of great-great-grandchildren would number 37. And they would have 3 great-great-great-grandchildren. The family of Clarice and Oren now numbers at 122. Add to that the current and deceased spouses and 6 step-children, and this line of the family numbers 174.

CHAPTER ELEVEN:

The Family of Chloe & Cloid Calvin

James and Margaret completed their family with the birth of a second daughter. Chloe Ida Glascock was born on December 31st—the last day of the year—in 1903. Peace between the National and American Leagues in baseball had been declared that year. The "teddy bear," in honor of President Roosevelt, was introduced. A drought actually caused Niagara Falls to run dry for a short time. Perhaps the biggest news of the year came that December as well. In Kitty Hawk, North Carolina, two brothers, Orville and Wilbur Wright actually flew.

Chloe was born in the midst of an extremely cold winter. It was so cold that quilts were hung across every doorway. Grandma Maggie fussed at everyone each time they went out for fear that baby Chloe might catch pneumonia.

Chloe grew up as the youngest of a rural farm family in Southern Boone County. While the pace of life was picking up across America, life on small, rural farms in Mid-America really hadn't changed much over the past couple of decades. Indeed, the pace of life would remain fairly constant for another twenty to thirty years. Chloe did her share of the chores, helping her mother and older sister. But when needed the girls could and did help out in the fields and with the livestock.

Besides the work on the farm, Chloe played, went to school, and did the normal things that young girls did in rural America at the time. She grew into a young lady. Her life revolved around the farm, around Wilton, and around Ashland. But eventually her world began to include a young man—Cloid Calvin. Cloid was born in 1890, and was some thirteen years older than Chloe. So there was a bit of a difference in their ages.

Chloe and Cloid were married on the 29th of March in 1929. They lived and worked on the farm with his mother and brothers for several years. They then moved to the Wilton-Easley bottoms close to the river. Before many more years slipped by, they bought a log cabin from Chloe's brother John to make a new home. Cloid raised watermelons, tobacco, and sugar cane in those early years. He always seemed to have a strawberry patch and a peach orchard. Cloid worked at the rock wool plant in Easley for several years while he farmed. Later in life, he went to work for the University of Missouri and farmed on a part time basis. He would retire from the University, but continued to raise watermelons. In addition to keeping the home, Chloe tended the garden and canned produce for the winter.

Chloe was, like most every woman in the Glascock family, an expert quilter. She pieced quilt blocks, pulled out the quilting frames and pieced them together. She pieced her quilts together completely by hand. Quilts were necessary during the winter months to keep warm in bed overnight. But they were much more than just something functional—they were also works of art and expressions of the love and care of the quilter.

As Chloe and Cloid approached their first anniversary together, they welcomed their first child into their family. Maggie Luetta Calvin was born on March 13th, 1930. Within a couple of more years, their first son was born, Eldon Hartley Calvin, who arrived in this world on the 29th of September, 1932. Both Maggie and Eldon were probably born on the farm of Cloid's parents.

By the time their third child arrived, Chloe and Cloid were living in the Wilton and Easley bottoms. There Jimmy Joe Calvin was born, on July 25th, 1937. Chloe and Cloid rounded out their family with another daughter, Marilyn Joyce Calvin, who arrived on July 10th, 1940. By that time, Chloe and Cloid were living in the log cabin they had purchased from Chloe's brother, John.

Life on the farm was always a challenge, but during the Great Depression rural life was often hard and severe. Nonetheless, Chloe and Cloid were up to the challenge and raised their family tending garden and growing watermelons in the Missouri River bottoms. The kids grew up and began to start families of their own.

Chloe was active in the American War Mothers organization for many years along with her sister, Clarice. She served as an officer at the same time that Clarice was president.

Maggie was the first to marry, as she wed Buford Allen Crane on July 19th, 1948. Chloe and Cloid's first grandchild came along a few years later when Maggie and Buford welcomed Keith Allen Crane into their family, on March 30, 1954, just a day after his grandparent's 25th wedding anniversary. Maggie and Buford would add a granddaughter to Chloe and Cloid's family in 1957, when Karen Elaine Crane was born that June 25th. Two years later, another grandson, Kevin Kent Crane arrived on September 26th, 1959, the day before the reunion that year.

During this time, Chloe and Cloid were also kept busy with the marriages of their other three children.

Eldon married Shirley Ann Gronemeier on July 14th, 1956. They added another two grandsons to the family, with the births of Hartley Eugene on April 27th, 1957, and Vincent Cloid on October 1st, of 1958.

Jimmy Joe was married to Evadna Ruth (Debbie) Christy on May 14th, 1958. Jimmy Joe and Debbie began their family in 1961. Their  first child, a daughter named Teresa Jo, was born and died on January 14th. Later that year, their first son, and Chloe and Cloid's fifth grandson was born on December 20th, 1961. He was named Douglas Joe Calvin. Jimmy Joe and Debbie would add another grandson and granddaughter to Chloe and Cloid's family. Daniel Dean was born on September 17th, 1963. Denise Marchelle arrived on the 14th of December, in 1968.

Later that same year, on September 5th, Marilyn married Howard Eugene Bennett. Marilyn and Gene added a grandson and a granddaughter to the family. Christopher Joel Bennett came early in 1968, on January 22nd. Andrea Jean Bennett was born two years later, on the 25th of September, 1970. With her arrival, Chloe and Cloid's family extended through their four children to include seven grandsons and four granddaughters.

Chloe and Cloid marked their fiftieth wedding anniversary on March 29th of 1979. All of their children and grandchildren were in attendance. It was an occasion attended by many families and friends at the celebration at Woodcrest Church.

By the next year however, both Chloe and Cloid were in poor health. Chloe suffered a stroke in January of 1980. After a short hospital stay, she returned home and passed away on March 10th of 1980 from complications with her heart and diabetes. Cloid grieved that he had married a younger woman so that she would outlive him. Cloid followed her only fourteen days later, as he died on the 24th of March. Several in family remain convinced that he died from a broken heart as much as anything else. They were both laid to rest, side-by-side, in Woodcrest Cemetery in Ashland.

Chloe was also, perhaps, the family poet. Her dairy, in which she recorded poems for all sorts of occasions, is one of the prize possessions today of her daughter, Marilyn.

THE FAMILY OF MAGGIE AND BUFORD

 Maggie Luetta Calvin was the first child of Chloe and Cloid, born in March of 1930. She grew up on the farm and married Buford Allen Crane on July 10th, 1948. They waited a few years to begin their family, welcoming their oldest son, Keith Allen, on March 30th of 1954. Daughter Karen Elaine followed on the 25th of June in 1957. Their youngest, Kevin Kent, arrived on September 26th, 1959.

Maggie Lu was a stay-at-home mom during the younger years of her children's lives. As they grew older she baby-sat for several years, before going to work for the University of Missouri. She would eventually retire from the University.

Buford worked as a pressman for both the Columbia Tribune and Columbia Missourian newspapers. He then went to work for Inland Printing and installed printing presses all across the country.

Maggie and Buford became grandparents for the first time with the arrival of Keith's daughter, Amanda Marie Crane on November 13th, 1975. Keith would add a grandson as well, with the birth of Ryan Allen Crane on June 11th, 1979.

Amanda would give Maggie and Buford their great-grandson. Jonathan Crane was born on May 14th, 2002.

Karen Elaine married Robert Johnson on December 17th, 1976. They would have a daughter and a son. Jenifer Kristine Johnson was born on July 5th, 1979. Their son, Jason Adam Johnson, was born on July 20th, 1982.

Jenifer has two daughters and two sons. Sebrina Michelle Johnson-Basco was born on the 28th of December, in 1996. This was the first grandchild of Karen and Robert. Cheyenne

Maree Johnson arrived on March 26th, 2002. Kaleb Lee Swickard arrived on January 19th, 2005. His younger brother, Broc Maximus Swickard, was born August 22nd, 2006.

Jason married Ashley Forbes on the 16th of May, 2009. They have a daughter, Piper Alivia Johnson, born on April 7th, 2007.

Buford became ill while working and was diagnosed with cancer. He died on November 22nd, 1984, at the age of 56. He was laid to rest at Memorial Cemetery in Columbia. Maggie Lu would have many productive years left to live and enjoys her grandchildren and great-grandchildren to this day.

FAMILY OF ELDON AND SHIRLEY ANN

Eldon Hartley was the oldest son of Chloe and Cloid, coming into this world on September 29th of 1932. When he became a young man, he would serve in the U.S. Navy for several years. He married Shirley Ann Gronemeier on July 14th, 1956. Eldon and Shirley shared the same birthday.

Eldon was also a pressman like his brother-in-law. He worked at Artcraft Printing when he first came home from the Navy. An accident on the job cost Eldon a couple of fingers, but he continued working. He worked at American Press for a while, and then went to work for the University of Missouri.

Shirley worked for the GTE telephone company and then the University of Missouri. She would retire from the University, though she would continue to work part-time.

Eldon and Shirley added two sons to the family. Hartley Eugene Calvin was born on April 27th, 1957. Younger brother Vincent Cloid Calvin arrived on the 1st of October, 1958.

Hartley married Sharon Calvin on August 17th, 1985. Their marriage immediately added two stepchildren into the family. James K. Hess, born on November 13th, 1986 and Marsha June Hess, born on February 12th, 1997, joined the family with the marriage of Hartley and Sharon.

James married Teresa Bobbit on March 17th, 2001. This union also brought three new step-children into the family. Allen Bobbit, born on November 13th, 1986, Chris Sweezer, born July 4th, 1988, and Kim Bobbit, born on August 5th, 1991, joined the family with their mother.

Kim brought Hartley and Sharon their first grandchild with the birth of Hayden Bobbit on October 10th, 2011. Chris Sweezer was married to Tiffany Westhoff and their son, Benjamin, became the second grandson with his birth on April 18th, 2012.

Vincent added a grandson and a granddaughter to Eldon and Shirley's family. Tamara Calvin was born on May 15th, 1987, followed by Brandon Calvin, who arrived on April 21st, 1989. Brandon was recently married to Faith Hurst, on March 22nd, 2011. Tamara gave birth to Conner David Calvin Johnson on August 8th, 2012.

Eldon was diagnosed with cancer—Lymphoma to be exact—though the doctor's prognosis considered it treatable. It was not to be however, as Eldon passed away on May 14th, 2006—Mother's Day.

Eldon and Shirley would have received their Golden Anniversary in July of that year, and Eldon's death left them two months short of that goal. Their children however were determined that they would still celebrate, so in February of that year, just a couple of months before Eldon's death, they threw a surprise 50th Anniversary Party, honoring their parents.

Shirley has had many years left, and works part-time while enjoying her family.

FAMILY OF JIMMY JOE AND DEBBIE

Jimmy Joe was the second son and third child of Chloe and Cloid. He was born in the

summer of 1937, on July 25th. Jimmy Joe grew up and followed his brother into military service. He was inducted into the U.S. Air Force in 1957, and served for a four year hitch. Among his duty stations was a stint at Tullee Air Base in Greenland, making him the only known family member to live on that island!

While in the service, he married Evadna Ruth Christy, who went by "Debbie." They wed on May 14th, 1958. Their oldest daughter, Teresa Jo, was born while Jimmy Joe was stationed at Whiteman Air Force Base. She was born January 14th, 1961. Unfortunately she died at birth from complications and was laid to rest at Goshen Cemetery. Jimmy Joe and Debbie lived in Sedalia at the time.

Jimmy Joe left the service that summer, and he and Debbie had a second child, Douglas Joe Calvin, born on December 20th, 1961. A second son followed about two years later, when Daniel Dean Calvin arrived on the 17th of September, 1963. They added another daughter, Denise Marchelle, born December 14th, 1968. Jimmy Joe and Debbie raised their family around Ashland.

Jimmy Joe joined the Teamsters Union and drove for several different companies, including a stint at the Callaway Nuclear Power Plant. He then went to work at Wren's Garage as a mechanic before retiring. Not happy with just sitting at home, Jimmy Joe took a job delivering nuclear medicine from a company based in Ashland.

Debbie worked at several places and retired from ABB in north Jefferson City.

Daniel married Cheryl West and gave Jimmy Joe and Debbie a grandson and a granddaughter. Hailey Nicole Calvin was born on July 6th, 1995. Her brother, Hayden Michael Calvin, arrived on April 26th, 1998. After Daniel and Cheryl divorced, Daniel remarried, wedding Libby Morrell on June 19th, 2007. That union also brought a step-daughter, Bria Michelle Irvin, born May 15th, 1998 and a step-son, Kaid Michael Irvin, born February 14th, 1998, into the family.

Denise married Earl Allan Winger on December 18th, 1993. They would have one son. Jimmy Joe Allan Winger was born to the couple on December 15th, 1994. Denise and Earl divorced, but then remarried several years later, on December 19th, of 2009. At that time Denise gained two new step-sons: Sidney-Joe Alexander Winger, born September 10, 2001 and Jessie Allan Winger, born August 23rd, 2000. Denise and Earl and the boys live in Wisconsin.

Jimmy Joe and Debbie celebrated their Golden Anniversary in May of 2008. Friends and family gathered at Goshen Church for the celebration.

Jimmy Joe's health began to fail and he was diagnosed with cancer early in 2009. Jimmy Joe passed away on December 3rd, 2009—Debbie's birthday--and is buried in Goshen Cemetery. Debbie continues to enjoy her family to this day.

FAMILY OF MARILYN AND GENE

Marilyn was the youngest child of Chloe and Cloid. She married Howard Eugene (Gene) Bennett on September 5th, 1958. Gene was inducted in the U.S. Army in 1962 and they moved to Fort Knox, Kentucky, his first duty station. When he was transferred to North Carolina, Marilyn moved back to Ashland to await his return in 1964.

Marilyn worked for State Farm Insurance for many years before becoming as stay-at-home mom for many years. As the children grew up, she returned to the work world, first with Boone Hospital and then with Shelter Insurance.

Gene worked as a carpenter for most of his work life. He spent many years in the Carpenters Union before he went to work for an independent contractor. In his later years he worked for the University of Missouri and retired from there as a carpenter.

In 1984 Marilyn and Gene bought the Pierpont Store and ran it for over a decade, before selling it in January of 1995.

Their family would consist of a son and a daughter. Their son, Christopher Joel Bennett, was born on January 22nd, 1968. His younger sister arrived a couple of years later, on September 25th, 1970. She was named Andrea Jean Bennett.

Christopher married Michelle Yvonne Rippeto on February 14th, 1987. They would give Marilyn and Gene their first two grandchildren. James Cloid Bennett was born on September 2nd, 1991. Little brother Stephen Eugene Bennett arrived three years later on the 8th of September, 1994.

Andrea married Brian Anderson on the 22nd of July in 2000. They added two more grandchildren to Marilyn and Gene's family. Braeden Lyle Anderson arrived April 5th, 2003. Their only granddaughter, Avary Ilene Anderson, was born on February 10th, 2006. Andrea and Brian were divorced in December of 2011.

Gene and Marilyn also reached their Golden Anniversary. In September of 2008 they were honored at a reception at the Ashland Senior Center. Many friends and family attended.

Chloe and Cloid began a family that would, as of the 100th anniversary reunion, include 4 children, 11 grandchildren, 13 great-grandchild, and 7 great-great-grandchildren. This totals 36 direct descendants from Grandpa Jimmy and Grandma Maggie. Add in the current and deceased spouses and the 6 step-children that were added into the Glascock family, and the Calvin line numbers 55 past and present members.

CHAPTER TWELVE:

Golden Anniversaries

When Grandpa Jimmy and Grandma Maggie were married on November 10th of 1886, it's doubtful that they were looking ahead towards a golden anniversary. Like nearly all young couples, other more immediate concerns push the far off future out of their minds. There are houses to buy, families to start, and all the day-to-day details that draw our interest away from the distant future. Yet, fifty years later, Jimmy and Maggie Glascock stood among well-wishers, having achieved that Golden Anniversary.

Grandpa Jimmy and Grandma Maggie welcomed family and friends to their home on November 10th, 1936 to celebrate their golden anniversary. They received several gifts in their honor. Their children presented their father with a watch, and gave their mother a new dress. The grandchildren got together and gave Grandpa Jimmy a watch chain for his new watch and gave Grandma Maggie a necklace to adorn her new dress.

Grandpa Jimmy and Grandma Maggie set a bit of a precedence that day, as many of their children and grandchildren would also reach their Golden Anniversaries. In fact, the family can boast of a total of sixteen Golden Anniversaries over the past one hundred years.

It took until 1960 for the next 50-year anniversary celebration to occur. John and Stella Glascock celebrate their Golden Anniversary in November of 1960. Their daughter Dorothy and son-in-law Wayne Gilpin hosted a reception at their home. Dorothy made the cake while several of their nieces served.

Oren and Clarice Wren would be next to celebrate. The family and friends gathered at Woodcrest Church in Ashland on March 19th of 1969. They had hoped to hold the reception at Goshen Church, but the weather that March made that problematic, as Goshen Hill was nearly impassible in snow and ice. And, sure enough, a late winter storm did hit the day before!

The Pin

Originally owned by Matilda Rippeto in the mid-1800's, the pin has come to symbolize love and marriage. Her daughter, Margaret Glascock, married in 1886 and wore the pin on her 50th wedding anniversary - starting a tradition. Her oldest daughter, Clarice Wren, wore it on her 50th anniversary before giving it to her daughter, Oleta Forsee. Oleta and her sisters Fern McDonald and Lora Jones have continued the pin's 50th-anniversary tradition.

Clarice wore a pin that day that her mother, Grandma Maggie, had worn at her Golden Anniversary. The pin had been given to Maggie by her mother, Matilda Rippeto, and was now being passed down. The pin has since been worn by three of Clarice's daughters at their Golden Anniversary celebrations.

Ross and Lola Glascock would also celebrate their 50th wedding anniversary in 1969. Ross was adamant that the celebration be on the actual day they were married—November 30th. Fortunately that was Sunday, and friends and family gathered at Goshen Church in Wilton for the celebration. Their children gave a tie pin to their father and a family ring to their mother. Ross had gotten three pieces of jewelry for Lola, while Lola presented her husband with a golden wedding band. It was the first and only wedding ring Ross had.

It was ten years before the family gathered to celebrate another Golden Anniversary. Chloe and Cloid Calvin had been married for fifty years on March 29th, 1979. They were honored with a reception at Woodcrest Church in Ashland, with all their children and grandchildren present, in addition to a large number of friends and other family.

Jack and Erma Glascock were the first of the grandchildren to celebrate a Golden Anniversary. They had been married on November 30th of 1933, and gathered to celebrate with an open house at the Hilton Inn in Columbia.

1989 marked the next celebration of Golden Anniversary, with the fiftieth-year celebration for Lorane and Basey Vanlandingham.

Two years later, Pud and Bernice Glascock celebrated their fiftieth anniversary on November 6th of 1933. Pud would be the third child of Fred and Belle (along with Jack and Lorane) to celebrate fifty years of marriage. Pud and Bernice would quietly celebrate their Golden Anniversary with their family.

The year 1995 marked two more Golden Anniversaries. Lahmon and Mary Lee Wren were married on June 28th of 1945, and celebrated their fiftieth wedding anniversary that summer. They held an open house reception at the Optimist Building in Ashland.

Helen and Joe Smith had also been married in 1945, and celebrated their Golden Anniversary on November 23rd of 1995. They were honored with a reception at the Optimist Building there in Ashland.

Betty Jane and Ed Blythe would celebrate their Golden Anniversary on March 12th, 2004. They were honored at a reception at the Truman Hotel in Jefferson City on a Saturday night with many friends and much of the family attending. Ed completely surprised Betty Jane with a birthstone ring she had always wanted, but would never get for herself.

Oleta and Joe Forsee also reached fifty years of marriage in 2004. They celebrated their Golden Anniversary on with a trip to Washington D.C. with their entire family.

Jimmy Joe and Debbie Calvin reached fifty years of marriage on May 14th, 2008. They celebrated with a reception held at Goshen Church that spring.

That year, 2008, in fact would see four Golden Anniversaries in the family. Emma Fern and Perry McDonald would celebrate on June 8th, 2008, with an open house reception in their hometown of Caruthersville, Missouri, at the Church of Christ.

Marilyn and Howard Bennett reached that fifty year milestone in September, on the 5th of the month. They were honored at a reception held at the Ashland Senior Citizens Center attended by their family and friends.

A few days later, on the 20th of September, Lora Ann and Donald Jones became the sixteenth couple in the family to reach their Golden Anniversary. They celebrated with a reception for friends and family, and then a private dinner with their family and close friends.

Two other couples deserve to be mentioned in any discussion of Golden Anniversaries in the family. Fred and Belle Glascock were married on December 28th in 1910, and would have reached their Golden Anniversary in December of 1960. Fred however succumbed to cancer in the summer of 1960, less than six months from that fiftieth anniversary date.

Eldon and Shirley Calvin were also approaching their Golden Anniversary in 2006 when Eldon was diagnosed with cancer. Realizing that he might not make their fiftieth anniversary that July, their children threw them a surprise reception in February of that year, celebrating what they were so close to reaching. Eldon passed away on Mother's Day, May 14th, exactly two months short of fifty years.

The family has celebrated these many Golden Anniversaries, many of these unions have endured well past the fifty year mark. The current "record' is held by Clarice and Oren Wren, whose union lasted well over 69 years. Somehow it seems appropriate that they would then die within days of each other.

Two other couples also surpassed the sixty year mark. Helen and Joe Smith would celebrate nearly 64 years of marriage, while Lahmon and Mary Lee Wren would be married for over 62 years.

Jack and Erma Glascock, and Betty Jane and Ed Blythe, would reach fifty-six years of marriage, currently the fifth and sixth longest marriages among the family of Jimmy and Maggie.

Three couples who have celebrated Golden Anniversaries continue to reach new heights every day. Oleta and Joe Forsee are now in their 58th year of marriage, making them the fourth-longest marriage in the family. In eleven more years they can reach the milestone set by Oleta's parents. Marilyn and Gene Bennett are now in their 54th year, as are Lora Ann and Donald Jones—both couples were married in September of 1958.

Each branch of the family has contributed to this distinction. The line from Fred and Belle contributed the first three of the grandchildren (Jack, Lorane, and Pud) to reach this mark. John and Stella Glascock represent their branch of the family. Besides Ross and Lola, two of their daughters, Helen and Betty Jane, celebrated Golden Anniversaries. With Clarice and Oren setting the standard, four of their children also followed suit (Lahmon, Emma Fern, Oleta, and Lora.) And following in Chloe and Cloid's footsteps were their children, Jimmy Joe and Marilyn.

Perhaps it is also worth noting one other fact about the Golden Anniversaries in the family. Of the sixteen Golden Anniversaries celebrated in the first 100 years of reunions, six of them have come from marriage that occurred in the month of November. Perhaps it really is just a statistical anomaly, but it seems that November marriages among the Glascock clan stand a good chance of making that fifty year mark.

CHAPTER THIRTEEN:

In Service To Our Country

The Glascock family has had a long and proud history of service to our country. Many of the sons of the family have joined the respective branches of the U.S. military in order to safeguard the freedoms that we hold precious. Many of the daughters of the family have supported their husbands and sons as they went to some of the darkest and most dangerous corners of the globe.

When the First World War broke out, President Woodrow Wilson tried to keep America out of what many viewed a strictly "European" affair. Indeed, one of the primary rallying cries for Wilson's re-election was "He kept us out of war!" Unfortunately, as President Wilson already knew, America would be pulled into the conflict, and within just a few months of his re-election Congress declared war on the Central Powers on April 6, 1917. The standing army of the United States was barely 100,000 men at the time. A selective service act enabled the country to draft young men into the armed forces and close to 2.8 million men would be drafted by the end of the war.

One of those young men was Ross Glascock, the third son of James and Margaret.

Ross was inducted into the United States Army on July 5, 1918 and sent to Camp McArthur in Waco, Texas. Camp McArthur had been originally set up as the training camp for men of the 32nd Infantry Division, made up of National Guard units from Michigan and Wisconsin. When the 32nd Division was shipped to France, Camp McArthur was used for training replacement infantrymen for units already in Europe. Draftees from Texas, New Mexico, Arkansas, and Missouri gathered for basic training.

Ross was still at Camp McArthur when the armistice was signed on November 11, 1918, and thus did not see combat. He remained at Camp McArthur throughout the summer of 1919 and attained the rank of corporal that August. He was discharged in time for him to make it home by the birthday dinner in September. And before the year was done, he married Lola Sapp.

While the whole family awaited the safe return of Ross, his sister, Clarice, also waited for the return of her future husband.

Oren Wren was inducted into the U.S. Army in September of 1918. While Ross had been

assigned a status as a replacement infantryman, Oren was immediately posted to a unit which was preparing to head to Europe and the war. Oren went through boot camp and then found himself aboard a transport ship ready to head to Europe—indeed, it was leave port the next morning. Fortunately, rather than watching the shores of home fade behind him that next morning, he gathered his equipment and disembarked back onto American soil. The armistice had just been signed to end the fighting and thus ended the need of more American doughboys heading to Europe. He returned home within a few weeks and became part of the Glascock family by marrying Clarice that next spring.

The need for military service dwindled for the next twenty years, and the Glascock family enjoyed the same peace as so many families across the country. But the storm clouds of war were again building, now in both Europe and the Far East. The Second World War would officially break out in September of 1939, though America would manage to stay out of the conflict for over two more years. However the Japanese attack on Pearl Harbor ended the quiet and peace the family enjoyed. Many of the sons of the family know found themselves either drafted or volunteering, while many of the daughters of the family found their loved one overseas.

The first son of the family to leave for the war was Estil D. Glascock. He was inducted into the U.S. Army on January 26, 1942—not even two months from the bombing of Pearl Harbor.

Other sons of the family would follow. Perhaps fueled by the example of their father in the previous war, three sons of Oren and Clarice Wren went overseas during World War II.

Virgil was the next in the family to be inducted, and he left for the U.S. Army on November 11, 1942 as part of the Army Air Force. He was stationed in Europe and participated in the Battle of the Bulge in late December of 1944. Virgil told the story of a scouting mission he was part of. He and his company were crawling on their bellies when he felt a pull or a tug on his shoulder. He ignored it, it went away, and he completed the mission. Upon returning to base, he found a bullet hole in his backpack, with the slug still lodged in the pack. A German bullet had missed him, though not his backpack.

Lahmon Emery Wren left for the service on February 11, 1943. He was a cook in the 86th Army Infantry, the Blackhawk Division. The Blackhawks arrived in Europe in March of 1945 and fought in the final push to topple the Nazi regime. They were in combat for 34 days, seeing action along the Rhine River, in the Ruhr Industrial District, and on across southern Germany and into Austria. Their biggest claim to fame happened on May 4, 1945, when soldiers of the division captured the crown jewels of the Hungarian Empire in Austria. Like Virgil, Lahmon also had a close call. He and a close friend were carrying a container of water when they heard an artillery shell coming. They both dropped to the ground. Lahmon was completely unhurt—not even a scratch. His friend however was killed by shrapnel from the shell, and the water container was full of holes.

Lahmon continued with the 86th after VE-Day when the Division headed to the South Pacific to fight in the final push to Tokyo. Fortunately for the men of the 86th, the war ended as they arrived in Leyte harbor in the Philippines. They remained in the Pacific as part of the occupation force.

One of the good things about Lahmon being in the Philippines is that he would occasionally run into his brother, Thurman, who was serving in the U.S. Navy.

Thurman left home on April 24, 1944 and was eventually posted aboard an oiler, the U.S.S. Monongahela on August 9th, 1944 as a Seaman, Second Class. The Monogahela joined the Pacific Fleet in November of 1942 and earned 10 battle stars during the war. The ship participated in every major operation in the Central Pacific, including the invasion of the Marianas, the Battle of the Philippine Sea, and the Leyte campaign.

Thurman and the rest of his 250-plus shipmates would see action in the Surigao Straits, the invasions of Iwo Jima and Okinawa in 1945, and narrowly escaped a kamikaze attack at Kerama Retto during the Okinawa campaign.

That was not the only close call for Thurman however. He recalled a morning in the Philippines when the Monongahela pulled out of dock as another oiler took their place in the harbor. Before they cleared the harbor the fleet was suddenly attacked by suicide bombers. The ship which took their spot in the docks was hit and blown up.

Thurman wrote many letters home, but due to wartime restrictions could not tell the folks at home where he was. Undeterred by this, he developed a simple but effective "code" to let them know where he was. Janie, his sister, recalls that one time he asked if his pet guinea was doing well and if she still had her nest on the north side of the old barn. From this his parents understood that he was writing from the north coast of the island of New Guinea. Another time he asked if Janie was still teaching the middle school at the old Ashland "South" school. This meant he was on the south coast of Midway.

Despite the close calls to all three sons, Oren and Clarice and the rest of the family welcomed all three boys home safe and sound.

"Buddy" Glascock, Ross and Lola's only son, left for U.S. Army on November 14, 1942--just three days after Virgil Wren. In fact, they both left from Jefferson Barracks in St. Louis. Buddy eventually found himself in the Signal Corps, working in England as a radio repairman—and a good one. Buddy and a small group of other signalmen set up manufacturing shop to turn out custom parts for airplane radios. They did so with borrowed tools and equipment, and with improvised methods to repair and install radio equipment. Their work kept planes in the air when they otherwise would have been grounded waiting on parts. Their efforts were so important to the war effort that they were recognized by Allied Supreme Commander Dwight Eisenhower. Buddy was discharged on February 9th, 1946.

Murry Glascock joined Thurman Wren in the U.S. Navy; indeed the two were even inducted the same day—April 24, 1944. Murray was trained in base security and his service took him to several bases in the States, before going overseas to serve in the Philippine Sea Frontier. Murry was honorably discharged on May 23rd, 1946

While the family sent these sons to fight for freedom, several of the daughters waited on husbands—current and future—to come home as well.

Ola Mae Glascock, one of the daughters of Ross and Lola, married Robert Louis Taggart

in January of 1946 after he returned from duty with the U.S. Navy. Robert was drafted into the Navy in 1944 and was posted aboard the U.S.S. Adhara—the "Mighty A"—in the South Pacific. The Adhara was a cargo ship running cargo of all sorts throughout the Pacific theater. In 1943 the Adhara withstood a savage attack at Guadalcanal that required major repair work in New Zealand. The ship was back in business by late 1943 though, and resumed her duties. The Adhara earned two battle stars. Her most serious action was at the invasion of Okinawa in the war's final months.

While Esther waited at home for her brothers to come safely home, she also waited on her husband. Will Lewis, known as Bill, was a Petty Officer 1st class in the U.S. Navy. He spent the war in the states, primarily in Texas.

Janie's sister, Oleta, also had her future husband in the service. Joseph Forsee served in the 94th division of the U.S. Army during the war in Europe, seeing action at the Battle of the Bulge. He remained in the service after the war, and then was in Korea during the Korean Conflict.

Ola Mae's older sister, Helen, also waited for her future husband to come home. Joseph Clifford Smith entered the U.S. Army on September 14, 1942. He trained in Utah as an infantryman and served in England and later Germany. He stayed through the end of the war before his discharge. He arrived home in November of 1945 and he and Helen were married just a few short weeks later.

As the War against Japan and Germany concluded, a different kind of war—a cold war—kept up the demand for servicemen and servicewomen. The Glascock family continued to provide her share of young men and women.

Fred E. Glascock (known as "Juno") enlisted in the U.S. Army in 1946, and became the

first of the family to make the military a career. After basic training at Fort Knox, Kentucky, Juno was posted as part of the occupational force in Japan for the several months. He was initially discharged in February of 1948, but re-enlisted in April. He then began a career that spanned some thirty years. He was posted in various locations in the States, including Fort Knox in Kentucky, Fort Benning in Georgia and Fort Lewis and Fort Lawton in Washington. He also served many years at various posts in Germany and served a little over a year in South Korea in 1965-66.

Juno also served two tours in Vietnam. He was one of the earliest to be posted there, from July of 1961 until October of 1962. He then spent another year—from July of 1969 through July of 1970—again fighting in the war in Southeast Asia. He finished his career with his longest posting—six years—at Fort Leonard Wood in Missouri.

Bobbie E. Glascock also answered the call of his country in the summer of 1946, enlisting in the U.S. Army as well. His stay was much shorter (a little over a year) and took a completely unique route—he served as a medical aid man here in the states, primarily at Halloran General Hospital in New York.

It was about this time that Betty Jane, the youngest daughter of Ross and Lola, was waiting on her future husband to return from the service. Noel Edward Blythe (everyone knew him as "Ed") was drafted into the U.S. Army during the Korean War. Fortunately, he was shipped to

Germany as part of the occupation, rather than heading into combat in Asia. One of Ed's memories was a six-week winter bivouac, when no one in the company was supposed to go inside a building. It was bitterly cold and the snow was piled up throughout Bavaria. At some point, the company commander came around and asked if anyone knew how to type. Ed's hand went up, the only hand to go up. He was immediately made the company clerk and went into a nice, warm barracks! He always credited the typing class back at Ashland High School as serving him well. Ed made sergeant and returned after two years in the service.

Eldon Hartley Calvin went into the United States Navy on June 23, 1952, and did his basic training in San Diego, California. He was stationed on a troop carrier, the U.S.S. General A. E. Anderson, as a storekeeper. Eldon and his ship made regular trips between San Diego and South Korea during the height of the Korean War. Eldon was discharged after four years of service, on May 17th, 1956.

Jimmy Joe Calvin became one of the few servicemen to serve in the U.S. Air Force. He was inducted on August 1, 1957 and went to Lackland Air Force Base in Texas for basic training. He was first stationed at Whiteman Air Force Base in Missouri (and close to home!) Jimmy then did a tour at Tullee Air Force Base in Greenland—making him the first, and probably only, of the Glascock family to reside on that island. He returned to Whiteman to finish his enlistment, and was discharged July 31st of 1961.

The decade of the sixties saw America embroiled in our most unpopular war in our history. Military service was becoming increasing unpopular. Yet the Glascock family continued to answer the call of duty.

Howard Eugene Bennett was inducted in the U.S. Army on May 14, 1962 and headed to basic training at nearby Fort Leonard Wood. He joined the 538th Engineering Battalion and was assigned to Fort Knox in Kentucky. He stayed there for the duration of his tour, and was discharged in 1964, two years to the day of his enlistment.

R. Dale Lewis followed his father, Bill Lewis, and grandfather, Oren Wren, into military service. Dale was inducted into the U.S. Navy in 1963. He spent most of his two years in the service aboard the U.S.S. Shangrala, and aircraft carrier deployed in the Mediterranean Sea. Dale attained the rank of 2nd Class Airman.

D. Brent Wren, son of Virgil and Virginia, also answered the call of his country in the 1960's. He was in the U.S. Army and spent time in Vietnam during the war.

Bobbie Glascock, Jr. followed his father into military service, enlisting in the Missouri National Guard in March of 1969. He did his basic training at Fort Campbell, Kentucky, and Fort Sill in Oklahoma. He attained the rank of sergeant before his honorable discharge in 1974.

Rex Taggart joined the U.S. Army in the mid-1970's, attained the rank of SSgt. and served several tours. His was first part of the 5th Special Forces Group for four years—from 1976 to 1980. The then transferred to the 12th Special Forces Group until 1988. He travelled much of the world during this time and was involved in Iranian Crisis as well as a tour in Greece. Rex became one of several of the family's "second generation" military servicemen.

Hartley Calvin joined the U.S. Air Force while still in high school. Upon his high school graduation in 1975, he went to basic training at Lackland Air Force Base in Texas. Hartley then went to the air force school in Champaign, Illinois for training in electronics. He was then stationed at the air force base in Emmarode, North Dakota.

As many of the Glascock women did before her, Traci Wren married a serviceman, Michael Howard. Michael made a career in the service, joining the Marine Corps in September of 1979. He retired after more than twenty years in the service, in September of 2000. He was stationed at multiple locations across the United State, and in Japan.

Doug Calvin also followed in his father's footsteps into the military. He joined the army in November of 1983, being inducted on the 7th of the month. He went first to Fort Sill, Oklahoma for basic training. During his four years in the service he served in Germany, near Nurenburg. He then came back stateside to Fort Campbell, Kentucky, where he was discharged on November 6, 1987.

The fall of the Soviet Union and the collapse of the Iron Curtain ushered in yet another kind of war. With the demise of America's primary enemy, the focus shifted towards a war against terrorism. Action against state-sponsored terrorism became a chief focus of the United States military as the 1990's dawned.

Mitchell Keith Taggart became a third generation serviceman, following after his father, Rex, and his grandfather, Robert. He entered the army in 1992 and currently serves as in the U.S. Army Special Operations Command as a Chief Warrant Officer 2. Keith has been on the frontlines of the War on Terror.

Keith's wife, Melissa Lee Taggart, is also a member of the U.S. Army, making them our first and only husband and wife military team! She joined the army in 2004 and serves in the Criminal Investigation Division.

James K. Hess, the step-son of Hartley Calvin, also became a third generation serviceman in 1992, when he joined the U.S. Army on July 11th of that year. He served a two year hitch and was discharged in July of 1994.

Nicole Lee Glascock married a serviceman when she wed David Fleetwood Anderson in 2004. David is currently stationed at Fort Sam Houston in Texas.

Noel Edward Blythe, III joined the Missouri National Guard in the spring of 2004. He spent basic training at Fort Benning in Georgia, before completing Advanced Individual Training for the Signal Corps at Fort Gordon, on the other side of Georgia. Edward served in New Orleans in the relief efforts from Hurricanes Katrina and Rita. He then moved to the combat engineers and spent a year as part of K-For 10, the peace keeping force in Kosovo. Edward currently is a staff sergeant with the Missouri National Guard at the armory in Lexington, Missouri.

A grandson of Virgil and Virginia Wren, Derek Lenger, followed in the family's tradition of military service and now serves in the U.S. Army.

Sarah Elizabeth Howe married Jacob Martin Myers in 2008. Jacob joined the U.S. Army in February of 2006. Jacob served two deployments in Iraq, first in 2007 and then in 2009. He is currently doing a tour in Afghanistan and is a staff sergeant. His third tour of duty in the Middle East ends this November of 2012.

 The latest son of the family to enter into our military is Jesse Garron Long. He left for basic training in the U.S. Navy in August of 2012, at the Great Lakes Recruitment Training Center.

The Glascock family has consistently answered the call of military service for our country. Members of the family have been in every conflict since the First World War, earning distinction and honor for themselves, for their country, and for our family. And while many have served, and have been prepared to make the ultimate sacrifice, all have returned to the family safe and sound. God willing, they always will.

CHAPTER FOURTEEN:

Those Who Left Us Much Too Soon

The story of any family generally focuses on those who lived long and productive lives, and had a significant impact on the lives of many others around them. The story is often written around those the patriarchs and matriarchs of the family. Yet the whole story is never written by those who did great things and went to faraway places. Everyone contributes their part and has an impact on those around them—even those who left us much too soon.

Even before the first "birthday dinner" the family had experienced loss. The fourth son of Grandpa Jimmy and Grandma Maggie was Virgil Leland. Virgil was born in the late autumn, November 27th of 1897. In the July of 1901, on the 11th, Virgil died. The loss of young Virgil was not something the family dwelt upon, but a little is known. His death was said to be caused by "Summer Condition." What was "Summer Condition?" Probably it was a catch-all name for what could have been a host of maladies. Typically the one symptom associated with it was uncontrolled diarrhea, which would eventually lead to dehydration. It could have been caused by a virus or a bacterial infection. Whatever the cause though, it was beyond the scope of whatever medical care would have been available to the young boy.

When the family had gathered for the very first birthday dinner, Grandpa Jimmy and Grandma Maggie had their first grandchild, Edmond, the son of Fred and Belle, at the dinner. As the next summer came around, they could look forward to the arrival of their second grandchild, as John and Stella were to be parents. However their young daughter was stillborn on August 5, 1913. Despite the loss, John and Stella hosted the dinner that year.

It would be a quarter of a century before death would visit the family again, though again, the loss was of a younger member.

Ross and Lola's first child was their daughter, Reba Ethelyn, called "Pid," who was born on October 8, 1920. Pid was what was commonly referred to as a "blue baby." She was born with a heart defect that, among other things, did not allow her heart to effectively oxygenate her blood. Throughout her young life she simply did not have the energy to keep up with the other children. Pid, though, was determined, and was looking forward to graduating from high school with her younger brother, Buddy that next spring. But it was not to be. Today surgery would most likely be able to correct the defect, but that simply was unknown at the time. Despite her condition Pid certainly defied the odds and lived to be eighteen years old. She passed away on June 19, 1939.

The very next year would again see the passing of yet another young child in the family, as the first grandchild of John and Stella lived for only two days. Dorothy and Wayne were expecting their first child in 1940. That son was born on August the 6th, survived two days, before leaving this world on the 8th.

For the first quarter century of the birthday dinners and reunions the family had lost three members, all young and gone much too quickly. Unfortunately they would not be the last of our youngest members to leave us.

Marthetta Lane Gilpin, the ten-year old granddaughter of John and Stella Glascock, was diagnosed with a malignant brain tumor in 1956. Her parents, Dorothy and Wayne Gilpin, moved to Kansas City for surgery and treatment. They stayed for three months and then moved back to Columbia where Marthetta was a patient at Boone Hospital. Marthetta finally succumbed to the tumor in March of 1957.

Thurman and Fonda Wren were expecting their first child in the spring of 1955. Carolyn Sue Wren was born on May 2nd of that year, only to live a single day. Her fight to live ended the next day, on May 3rd, in Wichita, Kansas.

Jimmy Joe and Debbie Calvin were also expecting their first child in the winter of 1960-61. Jimmy Joe was finishing up his hitch in the U.S. Air Force and was stationed at Whiteman AFB in Missouri. Complications in the delivery caused Teresa Jo Calvin to be stillborn. Her parents brought her back to Goshen Cemetery to rest.

Mike and Kay Taggart were expecting their third child in late 1984. Chad Derek Taggart would be their third son. Complications in the delivery caused young Chad to pass away at birth. He is buried in Sacred Heart Cemetery in Florissant, Missouri.

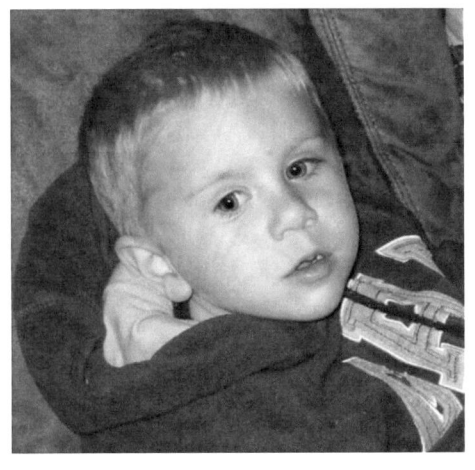

On December 6th of 2002, Cory and Carrie Beth Fischer welcomed their first son into the world, Boston Cory Fischer. Boston arrived nearly six weeks early and weighed just a bit less than five pounds. But he grew rapidly as an infant and became the pride and joy of his parents and grandparents. One of his first words was "refrigerator," which, given the family's love of good food, seemed somewhat appropriate.

Boston was 2 ½ years old in July of 2004, when he became ill on the way home from a trip to St. Louis with his "Grammy" and "Papa." Boston began having trouble keeping any food down, and his pediatrician began a series of tests. By the autumn of 2004 he began seeing specialists at the University of Missouri hospital in hopes of finding the cause of his illness. Originally he was diagnosed with Renal Tubular Acidosis, which went along with the earliest tests that showed too much acid in his bloodstream. Treatment though didn't seem to make much difference and Boston was referred to additional specialists. Then came the final and devastating diagnosis: Boston had a mitochondrial disorder known as Leigh's disease. Boston's life expectancy would be no more than seven years.

The family continued to seek medical help as Boston's health deteriorated. His parents and grandparents continued to care for Boston and make every day the best day that it could be. Others in the family pitched in to help, especially Jennifer Glascock Tade (the daughter of "Grammy" Bonita's brother, Bruce), Janet Glascock (who worked for one of Boston's primary doctor's), and Betsy Glascock Davidson. Betsy provided hospice care for Boston so that he was able to remain at home with his mommy and daddy.

Boston's fight came to an end on October 1, 2006 at the age of three years and ten months. He was buried in the Goshen Primitive Baptist cemetery, lying beside his great-grandparents, Buddy and Bodie Glascock.

The last member of the family to leave much too soon would be Riley Dalene Wren. She was the second daughter of Derek and Lisa Wren. She was stillborn on June 8th, 2002.

Each of these young ones left a mark on the family and created a memory in their brief time with us here in this world.

CHAPTER FIFETEEN:

Odds and Ends

Most of the chapters of this book tell big parts of this family's story. Yet not all stories are necessarily big. Yet they deserve telling, if with nothing more than a mention.

Grandpa Jimmy was a twin. His sister, Emma Elizabeth Glascock, grew up and raised her family along beside our family as well. This raises the question about twins in the family of Grandpa Jimmy.

Four sets of twins have been born in the Glascock family over the past 100 years. The twin girls of Emma Fern and Perry McDonald, born on March 9th, 1961, were the first set of twins since Grandpa

Jimmy. These granddaughters of Clarice and Oren were named Gayle Marie and Gwyn Ann.

The second set of twins arrived just 12 years later, another set of girls, born to Bruce and Donna Glascock. Jennifer Lynn and Jeanette Jo arrived on February 2nd, 1973. They were the great-granddaughters of Ross and Lola.

The third set twins would not arrive for over another thirty years. Bryce and Melody Arnold welcomed twin sons in to the world on April 24th in 2006. Payton Jefferson and Emery Leland are great-great-grandsons to Clarice and Oren Wren.

A fourth set of twins arrived in 2011, and again they would be great-great-grandsons of Clarice and Oren. Liam Morgan Lewis and William Murphy Lewis were born on December 6th, 2011 to parents William Floyd and Tami Schmidt.

While the family has produced four sets of twins, perhaps it is more remarkable that four other sets of family members have been born on the exact same day, even though they are were usually in completely different branches of the family. The first time this happened was May 2nd in 1955. Connie Jane Woodson was born to parents Judy and Warren Woodson. Over in Wichita, Kansas, Thurman and Fonda Wren's first child, Carolyn Sue Wren, was born the same day.

In 1985, two sons of the family were also born. Brandon Lee Bowden was born on

 December 7th of 1985 to parents Christopher and Christy Bowden. Meanwhile, Noel and Debbie Blythe welcomed their middle son, James Andrew Blythe, also born on the 7th of December in 1985. Both share Grandpa Jimmy's birthday on December 7th.

September 16th of 2003 would again see two new members of the family arrive on the

same day, and this time the two new members were second cousins. Ellie Elizabeth Helms was born to parents Shelly and Myron Helms. Her cousin, Hayden Ross Steelman, was born Shannon and Faith Steelman. Ellie's

grandmother is Brenda Austin, while Hayden's grandmother is Beverly Steelman. Brenda and Beverly are sisters, the daughters of Buddy and Bodie Glascock.

A fourth set of new babies sharing a birthday would occur on April 30th in 2008. Emma Grey Randle arrived to parents William and Kelly Randle. Emma is the great-great-granddaughter of Fred and Belle. Meanwhile Ross and Lola had another great-great-grandson when Mitchell and Melissa Taggart

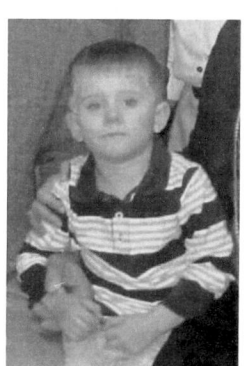

became the parents of Rex William Taggart.

No family gets as large as this one without a lot of babies obviously! Even early in the 100 years of the reunion, rarely did a year slip by with a new little one. By the 1940's, new babies were a regular feature at every reunion. In 1951, the family added four new babies for the first time ever. Just four years later, in 1955, five new little ones were born. The "record" then rose to six in 1959. A decade later, in 1969, we welcomed seven newborn members. 1970 matched that as well. The record climbed to 8 in the year 1975, and that was matched in 1985. We finally had 9 new babies in 1994. That record was matched in 1997, 1999, and 2002. Then came 2006! Newborns in the family for that year number 12—an even dozen. That still remains the record for the family of Grandpa Jimmy and Grandma Maggie!

As impressive is the number of new babies every year, the unbroken years with at least one birth is just as impressive. Or at least it would be were it not for one year—1971. Every year, from 1942 through 2012, the family has grown by at least one birth, except for 1971. The two previous years, 1969 and 1970, had seen seven new babies each year. But the well ran day, so to speak, for that one year.

The reason that the reunion is in late September is because, of course, Fred and John's birthdays were only two days apart, on the 24th and 26th. It would take until 1974 for any two family members to be born on consecutive days. That year, in June, Craig Taggart and Susan Jones were born on consecutive days—the 16th and 17th of June. This would happen another four times in the 100 years of the reunion. In January of 1999 Emily Marsh and Whitney Guinn were born on consecutive days, the 13th (Emily) and the 14th (Whitney.) In December of 2003 Gavin Blackburn and Boston Fischer were born on the 5th (Gavin) and 6th (Boston.) Interestingly enough, Gavin's mother was the same Susan Jones who was born on consecutive days with Craig Taggart in 1974. In August of 2006, Broc Swickard (the 22nd) and Grayson Glascock (the 23rd) were born on consecutive days. Finally, in August of 2011, Tiras William Blythe was born on the 16th of the month, followed by Delany Gregori, who was born on the 17th.

While births on two consecutive days has happened often enough, on only one occasion has the family grown for three consecutive days. That occurred in 1998. Hayden Calvin arrived on April 26th of that year. He was followed by Abigail Mulkey, born on the 27th. And then on the 28th of the month Spencer Al Sup was born. They represent the Chloe, Fred, and Clarice lines of the family.

A question that naturally seems to come up at this time is "just how big is the family?" The short answer is this: big enough to make it tough to count up! Yet with a little help it seems that the family sizes up this way:

- Jimmy & Maggie Glascock
- 6 children
- 25 grandchildren
- 76 great-grandchildren
- 136 great-great-grandchildren
- 129 great-great-great-grandchildren
- 4 great-great-great-great-grandchildren

Total descendants of Grandpa Jimmy and Grandma Maggie: 378

Add to that the 20 step-children that have been added, along with 155 current or deceased spouses, and the number of people connected with the family of James and Margaret Glascock grows to 553 persons. Of these 553 people, some fifty have passed away, leaving a family of over 500 strong as of the 100th anniversary reunion!

CHAPTER SIXTEEN:

Epilogue

Much effort by the committee for the 100th anniversary reunion went into this book and the reunion celebration. We were all continually calling family members wanting stories, dates, pictures and all the information that made up this book. I knew that we would never really get enough (at least from my point of view!) But we would get to a point where it was time to finally put it all down in ink and paper. And so this is it.

As excited as everyone on the committee was about the 100th anniversary reunion, there was also considerable trepidation. Would anyone else care? That was answered at the actual reunion itself. All the committee was overwhelmed at the response and the interest from the family. Some travelled great distances to be here. Others re-arranged schedules. In all, the count for the two days meant that at least half of the family came and showed up. That was rewarding to each of us on the committee.

But no one on the committee really was involved in this simply to feel good about this year's reunion. Rather, we all hoped—I at least hoped—that all the focus and all the attention would keep the family's interest in the Glascock Reunion high. For myself at least, my efforts were spent in hopes that this would spark and kindle new interest among the younger generations of the family. I hope that some of those from among the great-great grandchildren and great-great-great grandchildren of Grandpa Jimmy and Grandma Maggie would pick up the mantle of the family and keep the reunions strong for years to come. Thus, in the ensuing decades, everyone in the family would have the opportunity to know and understand their own roots.

This book was done in the memory of Grandpa Jimmy and Grandma Maggie, but a true memorial will come with the dedication of the younger generations to the preservation of their names, their history and this reunion. My hope for our family, and my challenge to them is that the younger generations take up this mission so that at the 125th anniversary reunion, when a next new family history should be written, it will be that much more deep, more rich, and more complete than this one.

To all of you, I hope you enjoy reading the story of your family as much as I've enjoyed writing it all down.